I0062108

STOCK MARKET INVESTING FOR BEGINNERS

MARKO BENUCCI

First Printed in Great Britain by
Obex Publishing Ltd in 2019

2 4 6 8 10 9 7 5 3

Copyright Marko Benucci, 2019

Marko Benucci has asserted his right under the
Copyright, Designs and Patents Act 1988 to be
identified as the author of this work.

All rights reserved. No parts of this publication may
be reproduced, stored in a retrieval system, or
transmitted in any form or by any means, electronic,
mechanical, photocopying, recording or otherwise,
without the prior permission of the copyright
owner.

Paperback ISBN: 978-1-913454-23-4
eBook ISBN: 978-1-913454-24-1

A CIP catalogue record for this book is available
from the British Library

Obex Publishing Limited
Reg. No. 12169917

CONTENTS

Introduction 4

Definitions... 5

Chapter 1: Investing In Your Future 10

Chapter 2: Frequently Asked Questions 23

Chapter 3: The Stock Market 34

Chapter 4: Stockbrokers And Trading Platforms 54

Chapter 5: How To Choose Shares 69

Chapter 6: Buying Shares.. 88

Chapter 7: Diversifying 126

Chapter 8: Analysing The Market...................................... 142

Chapter 9: Common Mistakes 155

Conclusion... 166

Introduction

Do you want to invest in the stock market but just aren't sure where to start?

The idea of the stock market and investing in shares, in general, can be daunting and many don't know where to start.

This guide explains, in simple terms, what a share actually is, the history of the stock market and looks at how you can start investing in shares from learning about the basic order types to setting up an account on a trading platform.

It considers how to choose shares and common mistakes first-time investors make.

If you are thinking about putting money into shares or just want more information on the stock market and how to invest, then this is the book for you.

Definitions

Alternative Investment Market (AIM): This is a segment of the stock market for small businesses that don't meet the requirement for a full listing, are more vulnerable and less secure for investors. Eventually, these small companies may grow to earn a full listing.

Bears: Investors who are pessimistic about a particular price or the future of the market as a whole.

Bulls: Investors who are optimistic that either a particular price or the market as a whole will rise.

Buy To Cover: Buy back shares that have been sold short (see below)

Company Risk: Risks that can impact a single company

Dividends: A portion of the company's profits that are paid out to shareholders either on a monthly, annually or quarterly basis.

Earnings Per Share (EPS): A portion of a company's profit that is given to each outstanding stock; calculated by dividing the net profit by the total number of shares outstanding in the market.

Exchange Price Information Code (EPIC): Unique abbreviations for companies, to make them easier to search for when purchasing shares. Also known as Ticker Symbols in the US. Some companies have similar-sounding names or issue more than one share so this helps to avoid confusion if placing orders over the telephone.

Forex: Foreign Exchange Market

Limit Order: An investor states a specific price they want to buy or sell at.

Market Capitalisation: How much a company is worth. Market capitalisation is worked out by adding up the total market value of all outstanding shares.

Market Order: An order to buy or sell shares with no time or price attached; whatever the share price is at the time of the order being executed is the price the investor gets.

Marketable Limit Order: An investor places an order for the market price. If they are buying and the share price rockets the order is cancelled. If the price falls lower when the order is executed, then the investor purchases at this new price.

Market Risk: Risks that affect all companies in the market as a whole.

Net Asset Value (NAV): The total value of investments in a fund.

Open-Ended Investment Company (OEIC) – Similar to a unit trust. (See below)

Passive Fund: A fund that aims to track an index as opposed to having a fund manager choose shares to invest in.

Peak Price: Highest price of a share

Put Option: If a share falls below a fixed price (the Striking price) on or at a certain date the investor can use the put option to sell at this striking price to limit any potential loss.

Redemptions: When investors sell out of a fund.

Robo-Advisor: Software that uses algorithms to find good investments based upon the investor's requirements.

Sector Risk: Risk that affects all companies in a specific sector.

Sell Long: An investor is selling shares they personally own.

Sell Short: An investor is selling shares that they

have borrowed in the hope that they will make a profit by selling at peak price and buying them back at a lower one.

Stop Order or Stop Loss Order: An investor sets a stop price; when the share price reaches this it is changed to a market order and shares are sold at whatever the market price is at the time of the sale being executed.

Stop Limit Order: An investor sets a stop price and a limit price. With a sell stop limit, the limit price specified is the same or lower than the stop price. With a buy stop limit, the limit price is the same or higher than the stop price.

Tradable Instrument Display Mnemonics (TIDM): Simply a replacement acronym for EPIC.
Unit Trust: Money is pooled together by a number of investors to form a collective fund which gives investors a diversified portfolio; investors buy 'units', and there is no limit as to how many people can invest or how much money can be invested in it.

Chapter 1:

Investing in Your Future

What Is Investing & Why Should We Do It?

Investing simply means putting money into a range of different assets with the view to increasing its value rather than just leaving your cash to sit in a bank account. There are lots of things you can invest in such as property, art, collectables, commodities, premium bonds and, of course, stocks and shares.

In the past, if you were to leave your money in a savings account, you would get a good rate of interest, but nowadays savings rates are very low. In fact, inflation is higher than the rate of interest, so money could actually lose its value in the bank. The argument in favour of investing is that, in theory, you should get a higher rate of return then had you just left any surplus money you had in an ordinary savings account.

Considerations

In reality, any type of investment has a risk attached to it, and therefore you need to think very carefully before you part with your hard-earned cash.

The focus of this book is, of course, investing in the stock market, and there are several things you need to consider before spending any money. Ask yourself the following questions and answer them honestly...

Can you Afford To Invest Your Money Over A Long Period Of Time?

You should only invest money you don't need in the foreseeable future. If you know you are going to need your money back in less than five years, then don't invest it. This is because stock markets go up and down so much that investing over a longer period means that if the market does dip, you will be able to ride it out and regain any money lost. Five years is the minimum but really the longer, the better. Some Financial Advisors will recommend ten years as a minimum period.

Of course, five to ten years is a long time no matter what stage of life you are at so it is also recommended that you have some sort of savings that is separate to your investment account. Financial advisors tend to suggest that this should be the equivalent to at least three months of your salary. This way if an emergency did arise, you aren't tempted to start selling stocks and shares prematurely as you could end up making a loss.

If your answer to this question was 'I don't want to put my surplus cash into something I can't access for a long period' then you may be better to pay more into your company pension if you have one; this is usually a type of investment, often stocks and shares, but is managed by someone else and so often feels safer.

Are You In A Stable Financial Position?

After you receive your incoming cash and pay all your bills and other outgoings, do you have some surplus leftover and are you free from debt? If the answer to both these questions is no, then my advice is *don't* invest. You should always clear any debt you have before using your money to invest.

Can You Afford To Lose Your Money?

Hopefully you will make lots of money in the stock

market, but as a beginner, you need to be prepared to lose some too. Don't ever invest more money than you would be happy to lose. The stock market goes up and down so quickly that it is not guaranteed to be a safe bet and there's always the chance that you might not get back the same amount as you originally invested. Hence investments over a longer period are recommended. If you think you might need to access your investment within less than five years you need to carefully consider investing in the stock market.

How To Be A Good Investor

The famous Economist and Investor, Ben Graham once wrote, *"The investor's chief problem – and even his worst enemy – is likely to be himself. The fault, dear investor, is not in our stars – and not in our stocks – but in ourselves..."*

Indeed, a lot of the problems an investor encounters is down to their own decisions and their attitude to risk rather than the stock market.

To be a good investor you need to;

Assess Your Attitude To Risk

This will depend on your personality as well as your age and personal circumstances. If you are in your early twenties and don't need the money you are investing until you retire, then you can afford to take more risks and therefore investing in the stock market is more attractive whereas if you are in your fifties or older, you will want your money back sooner and hence won't be in the same position to take risks; less risky options such as a mixture of government bonds and shares in blue-chip companies will be a more favourable option.

For example, if there were to be a stock market crash and the shares that you held fell to less than half the price you paid for them, if you are in your twenties and don't need the money for another twenty years you could afford to wait it out until the economy has recovered. In fact, if you were brave, you could even pick up some shares cheap which over the next fifteen years could steadily increase and in this scenario, you could end up making a sizeable amount of money.

However, in this same situation, if you were in your sixties, you wouldn't want to wait fifteen or twenty years for the markets to recover and you may be tempted to sell your shares before they lost any more value.

There are lots of online tools and platforms available which can assess your attitude to risk and offer basic financial advice and tailor portfolios to suit you based on the answers you give to a series of questions. This "robo-advice" can range from the very basic to the more sophisticated in nature.

Be Prepared To Make Mistakes

There is nothing wrong with being optimistic, but if you enter the stock market with the attitude that everything you purchase is sure to increase in value and you are going to be sat on a nest egg within five years, then you may eventually get a severe wake-up call. No matter how well you think, you can 'play' the market or no matter how many 'hot tips' you may have, there is no such thing as a safe investment.

You WILL make mistakes; this could be buying shares at too high a price, selling shares too early and missing out on their 'peak price' or it could mean investing in completely the wrong markets.

Throw into the mix the fact that these stock markets are incredibly volatile and unpredictable, and you may end up losing money. HOWEVER, mistakes aren't what count; making mistakes doesn't make you a bad investor, it's how you learn from them. If you are a good investor, you will learn from your mistakes by finding out how and why they happened. A good investor will learn when to stick with a share and when to give up on it.

Do Your Research
Do you know WHAT you are investing in?
Do you understand the risks you are taking?
Do you know how much returns you can realistically expect both in terms of percentage and timescale?
If you don't understand what you are investing in, then don't spend your money.

Don't Be Fainthearted
The markets go up and down on an hourly (if not more regular) basis. If you are going to check your shares and feel anxious and sick every time you see that they have dipped, then you are going to make yourself very ill. If you aren't happy to take risks or

are someone that will panic at any loss, then the stock market game isn't for you, or maybe you should go for a safer option and invest in the stock market but via a managed fund instead.

Trust Your Instincts

Some flexibility will be necessary; as the saying goes, there's no point flogging a dead horse, and sometimes you will need to sell some shares, possibly for less than you paid, but you shouldn't be selling and changing your portfolio every time you hear a stock market tip from a colleague or see some advice in the media. If you are happy with your investment strategy and feel you have a strong portfolio, then don't follow the crowd but instead, go with your gut instinct.

Be Brave

You will need a diversified portfolio so be brave and invest significant proportions of your money into different companies; some may be safe choices but mix in some less safe ones too in order to maximise your returns.

Don't Be Complacent

It is okay to have a bit of confidence in yourself but don't let success go to your head. You may invest in some shares and immediately notice they all go up. They may increase in value for another week or so, which may lead you to invest more money into different companies. You may feel you have some sort of a gift; everything you invest in seems to be doing well. Yes, there might be a few dips, but then they go up again. This may lead you to divert from the original investment strategy you had; it may lead you to invest more money than you can afford or you may just get complacent and stop checking on your investments as often. Remember; the stock market can fluctuate drastically, while you don't need to check on everything on an hourly basis you do need to re-evaluate your portfolio every now and then. Letting success go to your head can lead to bad investment decisions.

Advantages & Disadvantages To Share Trading

The stock market is gaining in popularity worldwide, and billions are invested in company securities and assets across the globe. For the companies who are selling these securities, the stock market is a crucial element in their ability to raise finance. Stock market investments can also form the basis for pensions and saving funds nowadays. However, like everything in life, there are advantages and disadvantages. It is worthwhile acknowledging these in order to form your decision as to whether you should become a stock market investor or not.

Advantages

Let's start on a positive note.

Dividends

A good reason for investing is if you choose a company that pays out dividends, it will give you an additional income annually during the years that the company is doing well.

Rate Of Return

Looking at bank accounts and the amount of interest they accrue these days in comparison to the rate of return you can expect to see on your stock market investments, it is clear that this makes the stock market attractive. For example, on a standard interest-bearing bank account you may receive 2% per annum if you are fortunate, and this isn't taking into account the impact of inflation or any taxes that may be taken off if you have a lot of money in savings. On the other hand, many stock market investors can expect to see a 10% return on their investments per year.

Asset Ownership

Buying shares can give you valuable tangible assets. Unless something catastrophic happens with the business, then these shares should retain some value which you can benefit from when you decide to sell them. This makes it more secure long term providing you pick good companies that have growth potential and sustainability.

Disadvantages

Now let's look at the downside.

Unpredictability

The worst thing about the stock market I believe is that it is unpredictable, and even the most experienced traders can sometimes get it wrong. Sometimes it's because the investor has read the markets wrong but sometimes it's just because the stock markets can change in a moment and nobody can foresee what was going to happen and because of this many people have lost a lot of money playing the markets. If it were easy and predictable, then everybody would do it and we'd all be multi-millionaires.

Risk

Oh, investing is a risky business, I guess this is linked to the unpredictability of the markets, but it can also be risky from the point of view that if you invest on a whim without doing your research, then you can lose money instead of making it.

Time Investment

In essence, when you are trading on the stock market, you are competing against others who all want a piece of the action and are there to make money. This comprises professional traders and experts who have the know-how, resources and knowledge of the stock market that you, as a beginner, may not yet have. This is why it is incredibly important to learn as much as you possibly can about how the markets move and what to look for when investing. This will require a lot of effort, trial and error and hard work but is worth it to try to protect your investments as best you can.

Chapter 2:
Frequently Asked Questions

This may seem a funny one to have as chapter two, after all, aren't frequently asked questions usually just placed in the back of a book? However, when people first encounter the stock market there are some things that they are unsure of so let's just cover them now.

What Is The Difference Between Stocks & Shares?
These words are bandied around and are often used interchangeably because they pretty much are the same thing. In this book, if I say stocks or shares, I will be talking about the same thing but if we are going to be pedantic than a share is the single smallest denomination of a company's stock. If somebody says to you "I own shares" you would assume they were talking about owning shares in

one company or they might say "I own 100 shares in Company X".

The word 'stocks' is more general and is often used to describe a portion of ownership in one of more companies. If you said to your stockbroker, for example, "buy me 100 stocks" they would assume you wanted to invest in a number of different companies rather than just one.

It is worth noting that shares can refer to a variety of different things as well including limited partnerships, mutual funds, investment trusts, exchange-traded funds and so on whereas stocks refer exclusively to corporate equities and those securities that are traded on the stock exchange.

How Much Money Do I Need?

In the past, it felt like only rich people could access the stock market and if you were seen as owning shares, you were considered wealthy. Many people believe that you need to have a large lump sum to buy shares but nowadays this just isn't true. In fact, you can purchase shares for as little as £25 a month. Yes, if you have thousands of pounds, then you can obviously purchase more shares and will have more choice over the companies you can invest in bearing in mind that individual shares can cost as little as a couple of pounds to a few thousand pounds depending on the company you want to invest in.

If you are looking to invest through a fund, then and Exchange Traded Fund (ETF) might be your best bet. As these trade like stock you can pick them up at a fairly reasonable price, usually less than £100. If you are looking at a mutual fund you will need more money, around £1000 is usually minimum.

Should I Invest Everything In Shares?

As this is a book about the stock market, you may be expecting a very different answer but actually no, you shouldn't put everything you own into shares. If you have a lump sum, say £20,000 then you should split this between different investments such as shares, bonds, property as well as keeping some back as cash just in case you need access to your finances quickly.

Investing in the stock market should be seen as a long term thing, and if you require a large sum of money for whatever reason, it is not recommended that you sell your shares (unless of course, they are at their highest peak) because if you sell prematurely you could end up losing out on potential returns in the future.

How much you invest would depend on your age and individual circumstances as well as why you want to invest. For example, if you were fifty-five years old and saving for retirement you probably wouldn't want as much of your money invested in risky shares so would go for a safer option of putting maybe 70% of your overall investment into stock funds and then maybe 10-20% in individual stocks that are more risky because you will want access to that money earlier than, say, a twenty-five year old who is saving for retirement. In the latter case, you may want to put a higher percentage of your money into individual stocks and diversify your portfolio but of course, you will be able to ride out any potential losses because you have the luxury of time if you weren't planning to access it for, say, forty years.

How Much Return Will I See On My Investment?
Well now, this is like asking how long is a piece of string?

Historically, the stock market annual returns that can be expected is around 10% of your portfolio. Therefore, if you invest £1000, you would expect to see around £100 return per year. If you invested £20,000 then you would expect to see a return of around £2,000. Similarly to accumulative interest, If you were to reinvest the profits, your investment would continue to grow, which means that your returns would grow exponentially.

HOWEVER, as I will continue to say throughout this book – the stock market is VOLATILE. Many people who invest in the stock market rarely get average year on year returns which means one year you may get more, the next you may get less. Unfortunately, it isn't predictable and is often influenced by external factors beyond our control such as company performance and the performance of the economy as a whole, so in times where people have a lot of money, many companies do well because people are spending this money and purchasing products allowing companies to grow. In times of economic downturn when there are limited disposable funds, share prices tend to fall just because companies aren't performing as well and people don't have the spare cash to invest.

You also have to take into account things like inflation which can reduce your return by 2-3% a year plus any charges you may incur on trading or dealing accounts. There are no guarantees, but it is likely that if you leave your investments over the long term, you will end up with higher returns accumulating over time than if you just invested for five years.

Take the above example; for instance, let's say you invested £1,000 and saw the average annual £100 return. If you take your money out after five years, then you will have a profit of £500 (if accumulative, it would be over £600 after 5 years) which although doesn't sound much is still better than the interest you would have accumulated had it been sitting in the bank for this long.

Let's say you invest £1,000 over thirty years however. It's still only three thousand pounds return, BUT chances are, over this period of time, you are going to be adding to it. Maybe you invest £1,000 a year or perhaps you receive dividends each year and reinvest those – over the longer period the more money you invest, the more returns you will get.

Should I Invest In Companies Myself Or A Fund?

This is a difficult one to answer. It depends entirely on your attitude to risk, your personal circumstances and the reasons why you're investing. Funds are generally the safer option because they are managed by an experienced fund manager. Another option is a Robo-Advisor and the third option is to just do it all yourself; picking stocks and shares that you feel are a good investment.

I feel that if you are new to the stock market then doing it yourself is a lot of hard work but it is do-able as long as you are willing to put in the research and the time to find investments that are going to bring you a good return.

Funds however are of course pretty much managed for you so, again, it depends on what type of investor you want to be. Read through the following statements and see which apply to you;

I want to invest money, but I would rather have somebody manage my investments for me rather than taking risks myself.

If this sounds like you then you probably want to invest in a fund.

I want to invest money but want to do it passively. I don't want to choose stocks myself, but I don't want to invest in a fund or have high fees.

For someone like this, a Robo-Advisor may be a more preferable option.

I like taking risks; I want to be able to have the potential for high returns, and I would like to be involved in choosing stocks and buying and selling myself.

If this is you, then you will most likely want to do everything yourself. This involves learning about the stock market and how to choose stocks and taking risks. It can be time-consuming because you need to know what to look for when selecting stocks and shares. To get started you need to set up a share dealing account.

What Is A Robo-Advisor?

These are becoming more popular and are financial advisors that use algorithms and mathematical rules to suggest which companies' investors should put their money in. It involves very minimal human intervention.

There are a variety of different Robo-Advisors; with each one, you pay the service fee which can be either a fixed monthly fee or a percentage of the assets in your fund.

It is super easy to get started with a Robo-Advisor;

1) **Pick Your Website**

There are many different financial institutions and platforms that offer Robo-advisors. As there are so many it would take half this book or more to go through each one and list the pros and cons, so my advice is just to do a search, look for ones that match the amount you are willing to invest and look at any reviews. There are some websites that recommend different Robo-Advisors depending on what investors needs are.

2) **Open An Account**

You will need general information such as your full name, email address, and so on, plus you are usually then required to fill out an online questionnaire about your investment goals. The Robo-Advisor will then look at this data and build a diversified portfolio that meet your criteria.

3) **Invest Money**
The software will automatically rebalance your portfolio, and some Robo-Advisors can even sell certain securities at a loss in order to offset gains in different ones; this process is known as tax-loss harvesting.

Is A Robo-Advisor For Me?

A Robo-Advisor is excellent for:

- Those new to the stock market who aren't comfortable as yet with making their own decisions and want to have it done for them until they learn more about it.

- Those who don't want the expense of a financial advisor yet don't want to make decisions themselves.

- Those with simple strategies; if you just want to do an easy allocation of 50% stocks and 50% bonds, then you don't really need a human being to manage this.

- Those who don't have time to actively manage their investments.

If, however, you prefer human contact and

would like to be able to interact with an actual person than a Robo-Advisor probably isn't for you. Some companies do offer Robo-Advisor services with additional live help, but this will cost more.

Keep in mind that Robo-Advisors don't tell you how much money you should save, how you should do this or give you any other planning advice; they simply invest your money and make decisions on your behalf. They also won't move investments or marry them up between other accounts either, so if you have multiple investment accounts, then a Robo-Advisor probably isn't the best option.

Chapter 3:
The Stock Market

A Brief History

Back in the early days of the British Empire, there was a great deal of money to be made if you had the cash to send a ship and crew to far-away places to search for luxuries such as silks, chocolate, tea, spices and other goodies that the rich folk would pay handsomely for. Of course, only the very wealthiest people had the money for a ship and crew and not many of them wanted to take the risk; after all the ship may come back empty, assuming it came back at all!

Merchants came up with an ingenious plan; why not pool together their resources to split the cost of the expedition? Each merchant would put in as much as they could afford (or at least what they could afford to lose) and on the ship's return, they would 'share' whatever came back with so if somebody put in twenty

per cent of the cost, they would get fifty per cent of
the expedition's bounty.

This way they shared not only the profit but the risk
as well.

Of course, if there were lots of people pooling their
resources together, how could they be certain that they
would remember how much they all put in? What
would stop one merchant from putting in twenty per
cent and then trying to claim thirty per cent when the
ship came back? Simple; they would write out
documents which stated how much each merchant
was entitled to. This is similar to the old share
certificates we used to use not so long ago.

Word soon spread, and people realised that the
documents they held could be worth money; why wait
for the ship to return when they could sell them? All
they had to do was find a willing buyer, agreeing on a
price between them and then handing over the
ownership documents.

Eventually, people started to 'invest' their money in a
variety of businesses, not just shipping and thus the
stock market we are familiar with today began to
emerge.

The first official stock exchange is believed to have

started in a coffee shop called Jonathan's in London when it posted lists of available shares and commodities along with prices. People used to buy and sell in there. This eventually evolved to a more official stock market such as the London Stock Exchange. However, just like when people started to share in the cost of ships and crew, the stock markets haven't really changed. They may be slightly more sophisticated, but the basis is the same; an investor will pay money for a percentage of a company and they will share in the company's successes as well as taking on a share of the risk.

Of course, we don't trade in cafes and public houses anymore; instead, much is done online and recorded electronically. Unlike the shipping merchants, you don't have to physically wait to be informed of what share prices are; you can go online and know virtually instantly. The advantage of dealing online is that commissions are also a lot lower now than they were in the past.

Paper Share Certificates

Until fairly recently you would receive a paper

certificate when you purchased shares, but this was more expensive and time-consuming.

Nowadays, everything is done online which is quicker and easier for both the investor and the investment broker.

Some stockbrokers will provide paper share certificates if you ask, but they as they will spend more time on preparing these, they will charge you accordingly with higher fees.

If you have any paper shares, then my advice is to convert these to online ones. Most platforms will do this for free; all you need to do is fill out a form and wait a few days for the process to be completed.

Dividends

As well as making money if you sell a share for more than you paid for it, you can also make money via dividends.

These are similar to the interest in a savings account; if a company makes a profit, then you get a percentage of it in the form of a dividend. This can be a one-off payment or can be more regular.

One thing to note with dividends is that in the UK

you have a dividends allowance per year. At the time of writing it is £2,000 which means that the first £2,000 you earn in dividends in any one year; if you earn more than this, then you are taxed at either 7.5% if you are a basic rate taxpayer, 32.5% if you are a higher rate taxpayer or 38.1% if you are an additional rate taxpayer. If you fall into the latter two categories then you must inform HMRC if you receive dividends that are subject to tax.

Shareholder Perks

You should choose an investment for its potential but there's no denying that perks are a nice bonus. In the past, these perks would be automatically given when people purchased paper share certificates and some platforms such as Hargreaves Lansdown, will pass them on but usually, you will need to contact the stockbroker if you want these perks nowadays. Examples of shareholder perks include things like discounts; for instance, Marks & Spencer would give their shareholders discount vouchers for various departments. It is worth checking whether you are entitled to any perks when you invest.

Scams

It seems like we can't do anything anymore without running the risk of someone trying to scam us and people may try to con you out of your money by offering you an investment. A general rule of thumb is that if somebody contacts you out of the blue and asks if you would like to purchase shares in a company, the answer should always be no.

These share scams- or 'boiler rooms' - often take the form of somebody cold calling potential investors offering them shares; usually they promise high returns and low risk yet these shares will be overpriced and worthless and that's assuming that they even exist.

There is no such thing as a sure thing when it comes to the stock market, so if it sounds too good to be true, then it often is.

Penny Stocks

The name is a bit misleading as penny stocks don't cost only a penny to buy. There are various definitions of a penny stock; one interpretation is if the share price is between 50p and £3, then it is classed as a penny stock. Another interpretation is that a company who has a market capitalisation of less than a hundred million pounds is listed in the penny stock market.

I'm not going to go into too much detail here because really you could write a whole book just on investing in the penny stock market. It is also not appropriate in this book because I wouldn't personally recommend someone who is new to the stock market delve into penny stocks until they have greater experience, but many people do consider them without any investment knowledge whatsoever because they believe they are cheap and safe.

The former is true; compared to some companies listed on the stock exchange they are very, very cheap however they are not safe, in fact, they are very volatile and speculative which is why they are so risky and not recommended for beginners.

You may be wondering why anyone would bother to trade in them if they are risky and the reason is that, as well as being cheap and thus offering entry into the stock market for people that don't have thousands of pounds of disposable income, for those who want to see significant returns penny stocks are enticing. For instance, let's imagine you buy shares in a blue-chip company like Apple or Coca-Cola. These are relatively safe options because they have proven that they can be successful even in economic downturns, especially Coca-Cola, that has a product that cannot easily be copied. If the price of these shares increased in value by 40p, it wouldn't give you a tremendous return but if you purchased a penny stock at 40p and it increased by 40p, then you have doubled your money.

However, you need to do your research thoroughly before investing in penny stocks. Unless you genuinely believe in a company or its product or you believe it is in an emerging market that will soon do incredibly well, then you shouldn't invest in them at all.

Forex

The Forex market is better for those who want to invest in assets such as currencies rather than wanting to pick individual stocks or funds.

The Forex market has become extremely popular

recently because investors aren't required to put in a significant amount of money and therefore it enables them to start trading and gives the potential for reasonable returns without the need for a lot of money. A lot of people have doubled their money within a short period of time.

The Forex market is less speculative than penny stocks and is tightly regulated. Information is freely available, so if you don't enjoy extensive research, then you may prefer to invest in the Forex market. That's not to say that you don't have to do any research, you should, but information is far easier to get hold of than it is for, say companies who are trading penny stocks.

FTSE

You've most likely heard people talking about the 'Footsie' or the 'Footsie 100' in share market discussions. No, they're not talking about a new type of onesie with feet but are referring to the FTSE 100 which is a list of the top 100 UK stocks with the highest market capitalisation. These companies are also known as 'blue chips', and some of the well-known companies in the world are listed here such as Shell, BP, HSBC and so on.

The name FTSE is derived from a combination of the Financial Times and the London Stock Exchange, both of who used to own fifty per cent of the index. Now it is fully owned by the London Stock Exchange.

Indexes:

FTSE 100 – This is a list of the top 100 and includes companies such as Vodafone and Lloyds as well as the ones listed above. It is changed every quarter to make sure it accurately reflects the top 100 companies.

The FTSE 100 represents approximately 81% of the London Stock Exchange market capitalisation.

FTSE 250 – This is the next 250 companies but still contains some big names such as JD Sports and Wetherspoons.

FTSE 350 – This is an aggregation of the FTSE 100 and the FTSE 250.

FTSE Small Cap – This is comprised of companies with small market capitalisation ranking from the 351st to the 619th largest listed companies on the main London Stock Exchange market.

FTSE Aim All-Share – This used to be called the FTSE Actuaries All-Share Index. It is a capitalisation weighted index and consists of approximately 600 of more than 2000 companies that are listed on the London Stock Exchange. This list is maintained by FTSE Russel.

FTSE Fledgling – This is formed of companies that are listed on the main London Stock Exchange which qualify for inclusion in the FTSE UK series but which are too small for the FTSE All-Shar Index.

The FTSE group set out requirements that companies have to follow, such as having a full listing on the LSE with a sterling or Euro dominated price on the SE Electronic Trading Service. They also need to meet specific tests on nationality, liquidity and free float.

What Is The FTSE Used For?

In theory, the FTSE should act as a gauge for the UK economic market but many people disagree with this purely because many companies that are featured in the FTSE 100 are actually international in nature. Many people believe that the FTSE 250 is a better indicator because a smaller proportion of these companies are international and that the FTSE 100 merely offers a snapshot of the UK.

Whatever your opinion on this, the FTSE indexes often are a reasonably accurate reflection of economic and international events and many traders will try to make a profit from price fluctuations in listed shares. Many technical traders believe that if you track the FTSE over time, you can get a feel for market changes and start to recognise when prices will rise or fall.

Rise Or Fall

Have you heard people say that the index is up by two points or the index has gone down? They are referring to one of the FTSE indexes. 'Up' means more people are buying than selling which causes share prices to rise whereas 'down' means more people are selling which sends share prices down. You may also have heard people say things like 'the market opened X amount of points higher' or ' fell X % in the day'. Usually these statements are followed by a specific industry or company share that caused this loss of gain.

Share price changes affect market capitalisation, which means that the overall index is changed in value. How much it moves during the day depends on the company's weight; a change in a large company's share price will have a far bigger impact on the overall index than a smaller company with a smaller market cap.

Why Do I Care?

So, you are probably asking yourself, why should I care about the FTSE?

If you are investing, then you should have an interest in shares and the companies you are investing in. Checking the FTSE will give you a good idea of the health of the economy as a whole and you will get a feel for how share prices fluctuate day by day, month by month, year by year, helping you navigate the stock markets better.

 It can help you make informed choices as to whether you sell or buy certain shares at a certain point in time.

Checking the FTSE can also give you a good idea as to how other investors are feeling about a company; if the share prices are down, then investors may be feeling worried therefore this could indicate that share prices are going to reduce down as people begin to sell. Likewise, if the share prices are on the up, it may be a good time to sell while investors are feeling favourable.

Why Do Share Prices Change?

Share prices fluctuate and the stock market can be very volatile, but what actually causes these prices to change?

Supply And Demand

Share prices are affected by supply and demand. In simple terms, if there is a high demand for a particular share but low supply, then the share price will be high because there will be more buyers than there are sellers. This means that you may want a share of a particular company but if it is highly sought after and most people are hanging on to them, then you could end up paying a high price. However, if there is a low demand for a particular share and high supply, the share price will be low because there are more sellers than there are buyers. Unless someone wants the shares you have, then you won't be able to sell them which is why if you hang onto shares when you shouldn't you could end up selling them at a price lower than you paid or you may not be able to sell them at all.

Investors' Expectations

When talking about share prices, people always say it is affected by supply and demand and this is true but you may now be wondering what causes this supply and demand to change? Why do some people favour one company's shares over another in the same industry?

It is all based on an investor's expectations. Investors buy and sell shares based on what they expect will happen to the price in the future. For example, if they anticipate company growth which in turn will lead to a positive price movement either in the company, the industry in which it operates or the overall market then they are more likely to purchase these shares. Likewise, if investors expect a company – or even the industry in which it operates – to take a downturn for whatever reason, they will start to sell their shares.

Dividends

Share prices tend to change when dividend announcements are made; if the dividend rate is higher than expected the share prices tend to increase, but if the dividends announced are lower than expected, share prices can decline.

Economic Climate

The wider environment can have an impact on share prices. If economic conditions are good and are expected to continue in this way, then investors will feel confident that companies will perform well, delivering substantial profits and are possibly more likely to pay dividends. This will create demand for these shares and the price will increase.

However, if the economic climate is less favourable, it causes investors to become nervous. Profitability can suffer when economic conditions are difficult and investors, especially those who are new to the stock market and aren't very confident, will worry about future profits of the company. This can reduce demand because people don't want to invest when the economy is in decline and share prices may fall if people start to panic and sell their shares. This means in times of economic downturn even profitable companies can see a decrease in their share prices purely because investors decide they want to sell rather than riding it out. Look at companies who twenty or thirty years ago were leading companies and are now either have closed down or are heading towards administration. People have lost confidence in the stock market and in companies at a whole when the economy takes a turn for the worst.

Bear in mind that some companies won't suffer the same setbacks as others. For example, those which are classed as 'non-essential' such as retail companies selling toys, furniture, clothes, jewellery, and so on, can end up going into administration during a recession whereas those companies that are classed as providing 'essential' goods such as pharmaceuticals can keep a steady share price during a recession. Let's face it; most people will still buy essential medicine that is keeping them healthy, whereas they won't be spending their hard-earned cash on a new outfit when money is tight.

Political Factors

Relations with other nations as well as government policies and initiatives can all affect share prices. For example, free trade agreements, or if a government is being favourable towards a particular industry and providing grants to companies in this area then it could encourage people to want to invest as they may see it as more secure than an industry that the government are steering clear of.

Interest Rates

High-interest rates can reduce demands for funds and lower the demand for shares. Lower interest rates can increase the demand for funds and therefore the demand for shares increases.

Company Performance

Listed companies publish financial results and trading updates twice a year. Most people aren't interested in them, but these figures do give an insight into company performance.

Companies are also obliged to publicly announce an event that could affect the price of its shares. This could be talking about a merger, a new product launch or a takeover by another company and these regulatory announcements need to be made through an approved regulatory channel before it reaches the public domain.

Press

A lot of people still believe everything they read in the media and depending on how favourable press coverage is towards a company, it can affect people's opinions which in turn can affect the share price.

 Just like a piece written in the press can make or break a celebrity, stories about a company can tarnish their reputation once consumers pick up on it, especially if they pass it around on social media, distorting the truth even further. Likewise, if a company wins approval, its reputation can be boosted which can attract more consumers, increase its sales and thus drive up the share price.

The bigger the story, the bigger the impact, but if

it's something that investors have expected, then it won't have much of an effect because it was anticipated already. You should read newspapers such as the Financial Times, which provides information about different companies because you can glean a lot of information from them. They can usually indicate whether people are going to feel favourably towards a company – for example, a story about a new product launching – or unfavourably.

Chapter 4:

Stockbrokers and Trading Platforms

You aren't able to ring companies directly to buy shares; instead you will need to go through a stockbroker – either a traditional broker or an online one.

Your other option would be to use a financial advisor or an investment manager who will purchase shares on your behalf; however, keep in mind that they themselves will go via a stockbroker to do this. Often the pension funds being used currently in the UK are done this way.

Charges

Many people don't even consider the expenses they will incur when buying or selling shares and they end up losing money. The main ones include;

Account Fee

Platform sometimes charge a fee just for having an account and depending on which one you use this could be an annual or quarterly charge or even a monthly one.

Some platforms will have a caveat whereby if you make a certain number of trades or are investing a certain amount of money, you don't need to pay the account fee. Before you sign up for anything, it is recommended that you thoroughly read the terms and conditions; otherwise you could end up paying money out unexpectedly.

Inactivity Fee

Again, this is usually just online platforms that charge this (as opposed to a traditional stockbroker) and is paid if your account is 'inactive' for a certain amount of time, that is, you don't make a certain amount of trades in a set period.

For someone new to the stock market who is planning to hang on to shares for an extended period, this can be both unexpected and unwanted. Some platforms now are trying to entice new investors by stating that they don't charge this fee but again, it is important that you read the terms and conditions carefully before signing up to anything.

Transfer Fee

If you transfer money out of your account, some brokers charge a fee to do this too. This can be as high as £25 per transfer so you may not want to be taking out all your profits every time you make some otherwise you could end up paying out more than you actually keep.

Buying And Selling Fee

Whether you use a traditional stockbroker or an online one, you will be charged a percentage every time you buy or sell shares. These fees can soon add up, which is why you don't want to be trading constantly. Frequent traders may be given discounts but unless you know how to make money successfully with short term trades or are just really lucky, then you could end up paying out more money than you earn because of the charges you incur.

Stamp Duty

In the UK you will be charged 0.5% stamp duty as well as an extra £1 on transactions. This is for buyers, however, not sellers.

Electronically, this charge is known as the Stamp Duty Reserve Tax (SDRT).

You won't pay stamp duty if you are buying;

New issues of shares in a company.

Units in a unit trust.

ETF's

Shares as an employee in the company you work for up to £50,000

Shares in an OEIC (Open-Ended Investment Company)

Foreign shares outside of the UK (Be aware that you may be charged other taxes in this instance)

I won't go into any more detail here but if you do want more information you can check the government information pages to find out more about the different taxes you could incur.

Capital Gains Tax (CGT)

If the profit you have made from the sale of shares goes over your Capital Gains Tax allowance, then you will be charged tax on this excess. At the time of writing the CGT allowance is £12,000 but is adjusted each year in line with the Consumer Prices Index.

It is up to you as an investor to inform HMRC via a self-assessment tax return. There are, of course, some costs you can offset against your gains but check these before you submit the return because some costs such as advising fees are not tax-deductible. If in doubt, consult a professional first. Many people will recommend you start with an ISA because you don't pay CGT on profits made from the rise in the price of shares that are held in this type of account.

Stockbroker Services

You have two choices when you enlist the services of a stockbroker. You can look at online trading platforms, or you can go down the traditional route. If you go down the route of finding a conventional stockbroker or financial advisor, then all you really need to do is a quick Google search to find one and they will guide you through the rest. You can find a comprehensive list of brokers at the Association Of

Private Client Investment Managers and Stockbrokers (APCIM).

Just be aware that good old-fashioned personal stockbroking services do tend to be far more expensive and can have a minimum trading fee of £40 or more.

Whether you opt for traditional or go via the online route there are three levels of service you may encounter;

1 - Execution Only

This tends to be online share dealing because with a traditional stockbroker, you will usually be given some advice. As the name suggests, an investor will buy and sell only. You will make your own decisions with no professional advice which can be scary if you don't know what you're doing. The advantage of this way of dealing is that you can buy and sell for very low costs.

2 - Advisory

With this option, you will be advised on what to buy and sell but the actual choice is down to you. (Usually, you will be given a full consultation and then you will instruct the stockbroker or financial advisor on what you want to do).

3 - Discretionary

This is a high service standard and usually, you need approximately £100,000 in order to get this type of service. However, you will receive expert management with a stockbroker choosing what to buy and sell on your behalf. However, it can be very expensive as not only will you have to invest quite a high amount you will also be expected to pay annual management fees which are approximately 1-1.5% of the value of your portfolio which, if you have a good stockbroker, can soon add up.

Many investors will say that these fees are too high; however, you need to consider that if you do have a vast amount of money to invest, will you make as much profit investing by yourself as you would using a highly experienced stockbroker?

Online Trading Platforms

There are many different trading platforms you can use. Traditionally people would have used a stockbroker, and you probably have visions of a trading floor as being lots of smart people dressed in suits staring at large computer screens and yelling 'buy' and 'sell' at each other as this is how they were depicted on television. Nowadays, most trading is done online and it is far easier to find and use an online platform, not to mention cheaper!

There are far too many to list here – in fact, I could probably write a book just on trading platforms that are available at the moment and so here are just a few of the most popular ones, together with why they are good and their downsides, to give you an idea of what to look for.

Hargreaves Lansdown

Established in 1981, Hargreaves Lansdown describes itself as the "UK's number one 'investment supermarket' for private investors. It is a very popular platform which has around 1,136,000 clients and is also a FTSE 100 company. It has won numerous awards including

The website provides tools and information such as calculators, research and guides so investors can make their own informed decisions. For those who need a bit of extra guidance, the company has a team of financial advisors and also offer multi-manager funds which can provide a diversified portfolio which is managed by a professional.

The website is easy to navigate, and there is also an app so you can access your account via a range of devices. They offer a variety of different accounts such as Stocks and Shares ISA, SIPP, Fund and Share Account as well as Junior accounts. It is possible to compare each one on the website to see which is the most suitable for your needs.

The downside to this company is the charges to buy and sell shares. UK deals can cost £11.95 per trade, which is expensive in comparison to other brokerage platforms. There can also be other charges depending on the account you use, such as for a fund manager so it is important that you check the key investor information before you make a trade. Hargreaves & Lansdown do offer international trades but, again, compared to others, the charges can be high.

A benefit for beginner investors who aren't planning to make a lot of trades every month is that it is free to hold shares in a fund and share account.

DEGIRO

Launched in 2013, DEGIRO has over 400,000 investors across 18 countries and has won more than 60 international awards including the Investors Chronicle and Financial Times Investment and Wealth Management Awards in the best mobile share dealing category for both 2017 and 2019 and the best low-cost stockbroker category for 2017-2019.

Its mission is to develop affordable services for investors worldwide and a huge selling point of this platform is that it offers lower fees than its competitors. For example, fees for a trade on the UK stock exchange is £1.75 plus 0.022% with the maximum charge being £5, making it one of the cheapest platforms for shares at the moment.

Of course, charges for international trades will be more expensive, but DEGIRO prides itself on its transparency and claims that all of its charges are listed on a fee schedule so you can calculate this before you complete a trade.

There are no monthly or quarterly account fees nor are there charges for opening or closing an account which makes it a good option for those who are new to the stock market and who don't want to be professional traders but want to buy and hold shares in the long term.

With regards to information, the platform is minimal which makes it a great no-frills option for people who just want to make trades without any additional support and if you are looking for market news or analysis you will have to go elsewhere and it is recommended that you do your own research into companies before you trade.

For UK clients there is no option to invest in an ISA or SIPP.

There is a mobile trading app and while it is very basic in terms of information, it is very user-friendly. Although it is an international platform, it is possible to place orders in your own currency which means you don't have to work out exchange rates or do additional calculations.

If you create a favourites list, you will be informed of price trends regarding the companies on your list. This list is synced between the website and the app.

AJ Bell

According to their website, AJ Bell wants to make

investing "easier for everyone", and like Hargreaves Lansdown, they offer a wide range of accounts such as a Stocks and Shares ISA, SIPP, Lifetime ISA and a Dealing Account as well as Junior accounts.

Their website and mobile app are excellent and have plenty of information including articles, market news and other information. If you are unsure about investing, they also offer a free first-time investor's guide and their website gives the option to compare accounts. There is also a calculator that enables you to work out the charges you would incur on each account based on the amount of money you're investing and how many times a year you think you would be trading.

Fees are relatively high at £9.95 per trade although if you make 10+ trades a lot, then this price per trade falls to £4.95 but of course, for someone who is just wanting to make a few deals then hang on to shares for the foreseeable future, this isn't as appealing as lower costs overall.

Accounts also have a 0.25% charge which has a maximum of £7.50 per quarter for a Dealing Account or an ISA and a maximum of £25 per quarter for a SIPP.

Saxo Markets

In 1998 Saxo Group launched one of the first online trading platforms, making international stock markets accessible to everyone. Like previous online platforms we have discussed so far, they have won a multitude of awards.

There are three account types on offer; classic, platinum and VIP. For someone new to the stock market and who is maybe only looking to invest a small amount of money at a time the classic account is attractive because it only requires a minimum deposit of £500. (To open a Platinum account, you would need a £50,000 deposit, and a VIP account needs a £1,000,000 deposit)

For UK listed shares under the Classic account, shares can be bought for 0.10% per trade (minimum of £8). For UK traders who want to change on foreign exchanges, there are different commission charges depending on which exchange they are using so it is recommended that you check before you make any trades.

There are also additional account charges incurred that you need to be aware of, for example, there is an inactivity fee of £25 if the account has been inactive for the previous quarter. This means you really do need to make at least four trades a year to avoid this (and time them so that each trade is in a different quarter)

There is a market data subscription fee if you wish to have access to real-time market data. Again, these fees are dependent upon the exchange, so for the London Stock Exchange it is around £6 per month. There is also a custody fee of 0.12% per year on accounts that hold open stock, bonds or ETF with a monthly minimum of 10 Euros.

Clearly this can be a costly platform for those investors who don't want to trade regularly, and it is an example of different costs that can be incurred which is why it is wise to do your research *before* opening any sort of stocks and shares account.

Can I Change My Stockbroker?

Whether you go via the traditional route or the online one, yes you can change your brokerage firm/platform. While many don't charge to open an account, some may charge to close an account or to transfer funds so check this before you sign up just in case you decide in the future that you are better elsewhere.

Chapter 5:

How to Choose Shares

Now you may be wondering, okay, I have set up a Stocks and Shares ISA or a share dealing account, but how do I choose shares? First of all, I'm not going to recommend specific companies in which to invest in; this is because what may be a good option at the time of writing may not be as attractive if you are reading this six months down the line due to the volatility of the stock market as well as political and economic factors that may come into play. Likewise, I could tell you to avoid several companies that in five years' time may be suddenly profitable.

What I can do is give you an idea of what to look for when choosing companies to invest in. I would urge you to do your research into individual companies

Price

Price isn't the same as market cap, but the price is important to you, as an investor. If you only have £1,000 to invest, you don't want to be spending most of it on a few highly-priced shares, therefore, the price of each share will determine how many you can have with the funds you have available.

Be aware that once a company has reached a certain level, they may 'split' their shares which means the price is decreased but the number of shares available will be increased. Not all companies split shares which is why some shares are priced far higher than others.

To see whether you are getting a good deal or to determine whether you should wait a while before buying shares in a particular company it is a good idea to look at historical data; does the price go up and down a lot? Has it steadily increased over time? Has it been high in the past but now starting to decrease steadily?

These factors will show whether you are getting good value for money or whether you are investing at the wrong time. For example, if a company's historical data has demonstrated that the company grows steadily year on year, then this is a good sign that it is performing well and could continue to do so. If however, the price goes up and down frequently, it may be an indicator that you should hold on for a short while to see if they drop again. A company whose profits have started declining over the past few years isn't something you want to invest in at the moment.

Dividends

Some people will say dividends don't matter because you make money by buying shares at a reasonable price and selling them at a high price and yes, this is true, but as someone new to the stock market you don't want to be attempting to trade immediately, nor do you want to be paying out more charges than you need to.

Dividends are important for people who want to invest and hold onto shares for a long period because it means you are getting a payment for each share you own.

Finding out which companies have the highest dividend is simply a case of doing a quick Google search.

If a company has increased its dividends or has been paying out dividends at a similar rate year on year, then this is a sign that the company is growing or has been maintaining its performance and these are the companies you should be investing in.

A company that has reduced its dividends or which was paying out dividends each year but then stopped for the last two years is one that you may not want to invest in at this moment because it could be a sign that they're not doing as well as they have done in the past. Whether they pick up in the future is yet to be seen, but I would recommend you monitor them for a while before investing any money.

You can also search for the dividend yield, which is worked out by dividing the dividend by the share price. Some companies that have been paying out dividends and increasing them for at least twenty-five years or more are known as the Dividend Aristocrats.

One thing to keep in mind is that some large and successful companies don't pay out dividends because they prefer to put this money back into the company; for example, Amazon does this. Other companies pay dividends because they realise that they don't provide a high growth rate in share value and want to give something back to their investors.

Earnings Per Share (EPS)

To work out the Earnings Per Share, look at the amount of profit a company has made and divide this by the number of shares it has sold. For example, let's say Company X made a £32,000,000 profit last year and it had issued 19,000,000 shares. The Earnings Per Share is £1.68. (£32,000,000 divided by 19,000,000)

Investors don't want to overpay for shares which is why they look at the EPS, and this can be a driving force when it comes to prices. Usually the higher EPS the more profitable the company is but be aware that it can be manipulated if a company buys back its own shares. The best range for EPS is often debated so while I would advise you consider this when purchasing shares to make sure you are getting a fair price; I wouldn't recommend that this is the only thing you consider when making an investment.

Market Cap

In a nutshell, the market cap is the value of all of a company's shares. Those that have a high market cap tend to be larger companies that aren't affected by bad news the way others in the same industry might be and therefore aren't as volatile. These companies have usually been around for years and have a steady growth rate and solid returns each year. For a first-time or beginner investor, these companies are good ones to start with, especially if they pay out dividends, as you can be confident that they should continue to grow and are not likely to be made bankrupt should the economy take a downturn. Examples of these type of companies include Coca-Cola, Proctor and Gamble and McDonald's.

Revenue Growth

Generally speaking – ignoring the whole dot com craze – most stocks go up if a company's profits are increasing and therefore revenue growth is a good indicator as to whether or not a company is successful. Don't be tempted to just look at revenue for the last quarter or the last year, go further back and compare each quarter to the previous. Look for whether revenue has increased each time or whether there has been a decrease. Small companies or those just starting out, may make a loss in the first year or so when they are purchasing equipment and have start-up costs but they should after five years or so, start turning a profit. Therefore if you are looking at a relatively small company or one that hasn't been operating very long, look at their revenue growth; if it is still at a flat rate after three years or is making a loss then you should consider the reasons why because it may not be a valid investment at the moment. That said, you may want to buy some shares whilst they are cheap if there are indicators that it will start to make a profit in the near future, therefore, look at revenue growth together with other factors.

For a company that has been operating a while, positive trend lines are a good indicator as to how a company is doing; if it has been a flat rate or in decline for the last two or three years it is probably not a good idea to invest without doing more research.

Proven Track Record

This, to me, is linked to the point above but as well as looking at the market cap, also look for companies which have a proven track record. These may go hand in hand but there are some companies that don't necessarily have as high a market cap as others yet still have a good track record when it comes to revenue and profit.

While there have been some success stories of people investing in small start-up companies that five years' down the line saw their profit – and thus their share prices – rocket, these stories are few and far between and, as a novice investor, I would be wary about ploughing my money into a new company that hasn't any solid statistical information to prove that it can perform as well as it says it will. Unless you have an insight into the industry or the company that others might not have I would recommend you start your investments with those companies that have a proven track record of steady growth and whose share prices appear to have held steady or grown over the years. Choose companies that have been around for at least several years or more. Ones that show steady growth patterns are far better than ones that decrease continuously with only a small spike now and again. Chances are these are the ones that other investors, including fund managers, are also investing – or are already holding stocks – in which is a good sign that the company is going to be around for years to come.

Do Your Research

I cannot possibly research every single company and tell you which are the best ones because, by the time I did and published it, chances are the stock market will have changed by the time you read it. Yes, the companies that are in it for the long haul will most likely still be good options but there will also be smaller ones that start to show promise.

Okay, it may sound like I'm contradicting myself here as I've just said you should invest in companies with a proven track record and I stand by that; however, I also believe there are some companies that are new to the stock market that are worth watching. Small companies shouldn't be discounted immediately but you should do thorough research and not just choose something on a whim because you like the company name or because the shares are cheap.

Whether you invest in a large company or a small one, one that has been around for years or a start-up, you should research the company thoroughly, look at what they do and how they are making money. I wouldn't recommend investing in a company that hasn't got at least some data to show, even if it's just a year or two of profit (or loss as the case may be)

Choose a company (or several companies) that you are interested in investing in and look at their historical data. If the company has been around for years then try to go back at least five or ten years, if you can look at the last fifteen years and get an idea of how the market as a whole, as well as the individual company you are looking at, has performed historically. The further back you go, the more information you will gain. For example, has the company been able to withstand a recession? How have they performed in times of economic downturn as well as times of economic growth? Has this company stayed strong while others in the same industry have folded?

While historical returns and dividends aren't a

guarantee that the company will always perform at a high standard in the future, it is a good indicator of whether it is high risk or not. For example, a company like Coca-Cola that is still making a steady profit and has withstood recessions as well as political issues, such as sugar tax, that has had an impact on the industry in which they operate, clearly is a good bet. On the other hand, a company in the retail industry that used to pay out dividends and turn high profits, that has suddenly started to decline may not be one to invest in.

Look At Analyst Reports

Brokers and investment banks often have reports issued by research analysts which give their recommendation on individual stocks; usually these reports have a 'buy' or 'sell' rating depending on the analyst's judgment of the share price and how they deem the company's finances. When you are doing your research I would recommend you check these reports, however, don't just read one but look at several; the downside to these analysts is that while they may be looking at the same graphs and data, they don't always agree so make sure you understand what they are basing their recommendations on before you take their word as gospel.

Don't Invest In What You Don't Understand

We're not all experts; I'm not going to say I understand every company in every single industry. What I can tell, however, is that I would never invest in something that I didn't understand, and yes, this means I may be missing out on some industries where other investors are making a profit but to me, this poses a higher risk because I wouldn't be confident that I would know when to sell and when to buy simply because I didn't understand the company or its products.

An example of this would be these small pharmaceutical companies that are working on developing drugs for various reasons. Some of these companies are showing promise at the moment but that is all; they are showing promise but not delivering any results, and they won't do until they have a breakthrough in their research. This could then go one of two ways; they could receive any licenses needed to sell their drugs and start marketing it making huge profits because it's a fantastic breakthrough and their stock prices will go through the roof OR they may not get the approval they need to release the drug or they could sell it without but never make any money. There is also the chance that they won't get the breakthrough they are looking for and abandon their research altogether. With the latter two scenarios, you will have lost your investment.

This is just an example; many companies have complicated business models that we just don't understand. My advice is that if you don't know what these companies do or how they make money, then it's better to just not invest.

Of course, how you spend your money is entirely up to you; after doing your research you may decide it's worth a punt and you can afford to lose the money you invest should the worst happen or you may have some insider knowledge that others don't have; maybe you work in the same industry or you used to work in it or perhaps you have a particular interest in something and therefore understand it better than others. I am not going to tell you what to invest in but I urge you to do your research and make wise investment decisions.

Look At The Industry

Don't just look at a company by itself but look at the industry in which it operates as well. This will give you an idea of whether a particular sector type is struggling at the moment and it can indicate positive or negative influences that may not necessarily be reflected on the share price at this current time but could be in the future. For example, looking at retail at the moment, many companies that in the past were performing at the top of their sector have now gone into administration or are on the verge of doing so. Why is this? What has changed and is it something that may alter again in the future or are all these companies at risk? What makes one company more successful than another?

Consider Your Own Opinions

When looking at the industry and individual companies don't discount your own opinion and habits when you are going about your daily life, as well as that of friends and family. For example, do you go out every day before work and visit a coffee shop like Starbucks? Are you choosing to eat healthily rather than buying fast food like Macdonald's? I'm not saying that Macdonald's is going to fold any time soon, how people feel about certain companies will play a part in their share prices. For instance, single-use plastics are a big thing at the moment and people are calling for plastic to be eliminated completely; those companies that aren't attempting to do this could be in trouble. If you know a company isn't interested in reducing its plastics use and you are against this then why would you want to invest in it? It is usually a good idea to invest ethically. Chances are other people are feeling the same way and if you ignore your gut instincts and your own opinions and feelings then you may end up with shares that plummet because everybody else has sold them.

Economic Indicators

No matter how much they would like to a company cannot control everything in its environment. Things like unemployment levels, interest rates, costs of production and prices customers are willing to pay, all have an impact on a company and its industry. Although they are seen as two separate things, the stock market and the economy are linked; usually, if the economy is doing well, companies are performing better and their share prices tend to increase. In times of economic downturns or economic uncertainty, companies tend to have lower performance, less growth and their share prices tend to fall.

It is worth looking at different economic factors and considering the impact these might have on the companies you are interested in investing in. For instance, at the time of writing, Brexit is having a negative impact on some companies because there is so much uncertainty around it. Hopefully, things will eventually pick up again for these companies but people are wary about investing in some areas at the moment. As an investor, you need to consider whether something like Brexit is going to affect the company and the industry before you part with your money.

Different Types Of Trading

When I talk about trading, I mean the act of buying and selling of securities such as stocks and shares in order to make a profit. There are essentially four different types of traders.

Scalp Traders

Scalping is done by active traders and is the quickest

form of trading with scalp traders sometimes only holding onto positions for seconds, or at the most, minutes. The objective is to make lots of quick trades with small profit gains, but because they are constantly making trades, the theory is that profits add up throughout the day.

For this style of trading, you need to be able to trade at the busiest times of the trading day where there is more trading volume and volatility. It can be a very stressful way of trading and to be successful, investors need to be able to focus on charts for several hours at a time and as this can be very intense, this type of trading is not recommended for beginners to the stock market.

Day Trading

Day traders enter and exit their positions within the same day as opposed to holding on to them or getting rid of them within minutes. The day trader will make a profit through frequent small trades rather than over the long term. For the day trader, the day will end with either a profit or a loss. Day trading involves taking time to analyse the markets, using fundamental and technical analysis to identify market conditions and trends and monitoring positions frequently throughout the day. It is good for those that don't want to get involved with scalp trading but who also don't want to hold onto stocks and shares for long periods.

Again, because it is so detailed, it is not recommended for beginners.

Swing Trading

Rather than trading within minutes or hours, swing traders tend to hold on to their positions for several days, sometimes as long as a few weeks to take advantage of short-term market moves.

It is attractive to those who want to be hands-on traders but who still want to hold down a full-time job and other commitments because it isn't as intense as day trading or scalp trading. Having said that, to be successful, you still need to put a few hours a day to one side to analyse the markets.

Position Trading

This is basically holding onto positions over the long-term rather than trading constantly throughout the day. This type of trading is looking to maximise potential profits from significant price changes. Position traders will still use technical and fundamental analysis to identify possible entry and exit points as well as weekly and monthly price charts to analyse and evaluate the market and to spot any significant trends that may be happening, however, they don't need to constantly monitor their positions on an hourly or even daily basis. For someone new to the stock market I would recommend they start with position trading because this gives them an idea of how it works and allows them to make sound investments without having to pore over charts for hours on end.

Chapter 6:

Buying Shares

Before you can buy shares, you need to set up an account which you will then use to buy (and sell) from.

The steps for setting up an account may vary depending on the platform you choose, but usually, the procedure is as follows;

Choose A Platform

Firstly, you need to choose a platform such as Hargreaves Lansdown, DEGIRO or you can go through a bank such as Barclays, HSBC, NatWest, Lloyds, etc. and set up a stocks and shares account. Many people prefer to go through their bank because they feel more secure, especially if they are new to the stock market however you may get a better deal elsewhere, so it is definitely worth considering other options.

Remember the main things to look for when choosing a firm are costs per trade plus any monthly or annual account charges and costs for inactive accounts or advice.

A good way to choose a platform is to look at the websites; many have a comparison table showing how their costs fare against other companies in the market. There may be a guide or a calculator to help you work out what your charges will be based on how much you plan to invest plus how many trades per year you think you will make.

Next, compare the accounts that the company offer; do they offer a share ISA or just a dealing account? Choose the one that suits you; for instance, if you want to avoid Capital Gains Tax (CGT) then you want a platform that offers a stocks and shares ISA. Again, many websites will have a question or two asking what you are looking for or how you plan to invest, which will help you narrow down which account suits you better.

If you think you will be more likely to make your trades via a tablet rather than a laptop, then it may be worth looking for a platform that offers a good mobile app rather than just a website.

Another consideration is whether you want to have a telephone option so you can make trades over the phone. Be aware that this is more costly than if you do them via a computer. For example, the Halifax charges around £11.95 per trade online, but if you do the same deal over the phone, it will be £15 per trade.

Finally, you may want to consider whether you wish to trade in international markets. For a beginner, I would personally recommend you just stick with the LSE for now and find a brokerage firm that offers low costs and allows you to invest in a variety of things such as shares, mutual funds and bonds as opposed to those that would enable more complicated trades such as foreign markets. Whichever platform you choose I would urge you to choose one that has an excellent customer service rating because if you do get stuck or have any issues, you need to be confident that you have someone on hand to help.

Choose Your Membership Level

Not all platforms will have this distinction, but some, like Saxo Markets, offer tiered levels such as gold, silver, bronze, classic. Be aware that a basic account usually doesn't have a minimum to invest or if they do, they tend to be low amounts such as £500 whereas more premium accounts tend to require you to put a higher deposit in at the beginning. Fees may also be different depending on which you choose. For example, a gold or silver account may include advice from a Financial Advisor or Stockbroker but the annual account fees may be higher to allow for this whereas a bronze level account usually just enables you to make trades without any additional advice.

Choose Your Account

Not all platforms will have an option, but some will give you a choice of opening a Stocks and Shares ISA (also referred to on some websites as a Share Dealing ISA), a Dealing Account, a Self-Invested Personal Pension (SIPPS) a Lifetime ISA or junior accounts. Which one you choose is up to you and will depend on what point you are in your life journey and what your ultimate investment goal is. They are all pretty similar, but it can be confusing. For example, when I say ISA you probably immediately think of a cash ISA which works like a savings account and therefore are wondering what it has to do with the stock market but there are also Stocks and Shares or Investment ISAs which are what I am referring to here. An Investment ISA has become a popular way of holding investments such as shares in individual companies, bonds or funds and are often recommended for those who are new to the stock market. If you make any profit either from an increase in share price or dividends you don't pay capital gains tax and you can save up to £20,000 a year. Just note that this £20,000 limit can be split between other ISAs so if you do have a cash ISA already and open an investment ISA then you won't get a £40,000 tax-free limit but will be £20,000 in total between the two. With an Investment ISA, you can take your money out whenever you wish.

However, it is worth noting that there is also a Lifetime ISA which has a cash or investment option and these are available for those aged between 18-39 years of age and you can pay into it until you reach the age of 50. The account will stay open but you are unable to pay any more into it once you reach this age. Again, with the investment version, you can hold shares, bonds and funds, and you can pay up to £4000 a year into it and receive a bonus of 25% from the government. However, the rules for this type of ISA is different with regards to withdrawal and access because you cannot actually access it until you are 60 years of age otherwise you incur a penalty (unless you are terminally ill or are using it to buy your first home) so you must read the terms and conditions.

A SIPP is great way to invest for retirement but again you can't touch it until you reach a certain age. At the moment it is 55 but it is always subject to change. If you just want to buy and hold investments, then this is a good way to do it but if you want to have the option of taking money out of it, then it probably isn't for you.

Open An Account

The next step is to open a share dealing account; this is a specific account that allows you to buy shares, so whenever you click 'buy' the money is taken from this brokerage account.

You own the money that you put in this account as well as the investments that you make and you can sell any shares you purchase whenever you wish to do so. The broker is simply the middle man between you and the stock market.

Opening a brokerage account is pretty much like opening a bank account; you will need to provide information such as your full name, contact details such as an address, email address, telephone number as well as some sort of valid photo ID, usually this will be a passport or driving license. This is where it can be easier to open a dealing account with your current bank if they have the option to do so because you will need to provide less information and usually don't need to provide current ID.

Link Your Bank Account

In order to deposit money into your brokerage account, you will need to transfer it from your savings account and therefore you will need to supply these bank details. Some platforms allow you to set up a sort of standing order where a specified amount of money is taken from your savings account and transferred on a regular basis such as each month.

Submit Your Application

Usually your application will be processed within a couple of working days, although it can take a little bit longer depending on how quickly your money is transferred from your bank. If you are setting up a dealing account with a bank that is not your own – for example, if you decide you want your dealing account to be in the Halifax yet your current savings account is held with Lloyds, you may have to wait up to a week for a password to be posted to your home address for security reasons. For this reason, it may be better to either just set up your first dealing account with your own bank or to use a trading platform such as Hargreaves Lansdown just to make the application process a bit quicker.

Buy Shares

Once your application has been accepted, and the money has hit your brokerage account you are good to go and can start trading.

What Next?

So, you've opened your share trading account, now what?

Remember that purchasing shares isn't a guaranteed investment and it is risky; I will reiterate here that you should only invest money that you are willing to put at risk because no matter how much research you do, nobody can predict whether a company will continue to trade, especially in times of economic uncertainty. Hopefully you should make a steady return but you do need to be prepared for losses too. When you buy shares, you need to do the following;

Choose The Company

In the previous chapter, we looked at what sort of company information you should look at when choosing whether to invest or not, therefore, I am going to assume that you have done all of this first and have chosen (or at least narrowed down) which company or companies you want to put your money into.

Before you click 'buy', however, just make sure that you are still happy with the company. A lot can change in just a few minutes in the stock markets and if you had done your company research before you opened your shares account then you need to double check that you are still happy to invest. For instance, has the share price changed since you looked at it last and if so, are you happy to buy at this new price? If the price has gone up, then you may want to hold off but if the price has gone down this is great, right? Possibly! You may be happy to buy at the new price, in fact, if the price is lower you may be tempted to buy more than you intended and if it's just reduced by a minimal amount then it's okay, but if it has dropped astronomically you need to find out why. A quick Google search of news headlines or checking any recent company announcements should give you an idea as to whether there are any new risks associated. For example, a new product may be launched which is why the price has increased.

Buy Your Shares

This is the easy part; if you are online, you should see the price that is offered and a button that says 'deal now' or 'buy'. Again, this depends on the platform but it is relatively apparent. You should get a confirmation or contract note afterwards.

Don't forget that you will pay a one-off charge for buying and selling shares. If it is a fixed amount, it is usually more economical to make larger share purchases than smaller ones. For example, let's say you were transferring £500 a month into your brokerage account and you wanted to purchase £1000 worth of stock in Company X. Rather than purchasing £500 worth of shares one month and then £500 worth the following month it would make more sense to just wait and invest the full £1000 in one go – otherwise you are paying two lots of brokerage fees.

You also need to remember that you will also pay Stamp Duty Reserve Tax (SDRT) which is around 0.5% of the trade.

Monitor Your Shares

I keep saying that you should invest long term, but that doesn't mean you should purchase your shares and forget about them. Yes, the company may do incredibly well and you could be lucky enough to just leave the shares in a company and wake up in ten years' time to discover you've made thousands of pounds return on them. However, it is foolish to just forget about your shares, especially in the times we are living in now where companies are constantly going into administration. You need to monitor your shares so that if the worst did happen, you could deal with it without losing more money than is necessary. Don't be tempted to sell every time the shares drop slightly but make sure you aren't just forgetting them otherwise you could wake up to find that a company you invested in has folded and you have lost thousands of pounds.

This is where it is worth knowing about the different order types we discussed earlier comes in handy; most trading platforms should allow you to set an automatic limit so that if your shares lose more than 15% or gain more than 50%, they are automatically sold. This way you can ensure that you have sold your shares when the going is good or that you have sold them before they make too much of a loss.

Monitor The Company

As well as monitoring the shares, I think it is worth keeping up to date with company news and announcements so that you can take control and make decisions based on the information you have. For example, when fracking started to come to the forefront, some people who had shares in oil companies realised that this was going to impact on share prices and many sold the shares they had in these companies. Low and behold, a few months down the line, some of these companies folded and those who hadn't sold discovered their investments were now worthless.

While you can't always believe everything you read in the media, if you get your news from trustworthy sources (check several different ones is my advice) then you need to take note of anything that may affect share prices; sometimes it may just be a sidebar about companies which aren't recycling for example, that doesn't seem important but which suddenly affects the share price because customers don't want to purchase from companies that aren't environmentally friendly. Other times it can be more obvious, for instance, if a company is struggling with its finances or if merger talks are being discussed.

Basic Order Types

Nowadays, many professional traders will use different mathematical formulas – algorithms – to help them make trading decisions. For ordinary investors like you or I, however, there are five basic order types that will be used for the majority of our investments. These are a market order, a limit order, a marketable limit order, a stop order and a stop-limit order. They can be complicated at first but it is important to have a grasp of them so you are clear what each one means should you ever use them.

Each order will be marked either as buy, sell long, sell short or buy to cover, so let's look at what these terms mean first.

Buy – This is pretty much self-explanatory; you – the investor – want to purchase some shares because you believe the price will eventually rise, and you will make a profit. Therefore, you will 'buy' or 'invest'. You may also hear the term 'buy long' used in the same way.

Sell Long – Unlike a basic buy option, you don't have a basic sell one. You either 'sell long' or 'sell short'. If you are using a platform that does just state 'sell' then this usually means 'sell long'. This is because 'sell short' is a more complicated way of investing and isn't recommended for novices.

'Sell long' means that you, as an investor, are selling

shares that you personally own.

Sell Short – As mentioned above, I don't recommend you ever attempt to sell short, but it is worth understanding what this is just in case you use a platform that has this option. I have known people assume that sell long or sell short mean the same thing and therefore have lost money on the stock market because they weren't aware of the difference.

Basically, if you are selling short, you are selling shares you don't personally own. Instead, the shares you are selling are ones which have been 'borrowed' from someone else.

Why? You might ask, and this is a very valid – and good – question.

The short answer is that it can be a good money spinner if you know what you are doing, but you need to have an incredibly good grasp of the stock market and how it behaves.

Those who 'sell short', borrow shares – usually from a brokerage firm – because they believe they are going to decline in price in the short term. They sell the shares they have borrowed at the higher price and when the shares drop in price they repurchase them. The investor will then return these shares and the difference between the price they sold them and the price they bought them back for is profit for the investor.

The problem is, of course, is that if the shares you borrow increase in price you will end up buying them back for more than you sold them for and therefore you will lose money and this is why it is risky and not for a novice investor. In theory, you could suffer unlimited potential loss because, of course, the price could drastically increase by an unlimited amount before you can buy them back.

In the UK an individual cannot do this in the cash market anyway; you need to either use the Contract For Difference (CFD) or Spread betting markets.

I am not going to go any further into selling short as I don't think it is relevant for a beginner to the stock market. If you did want more information on this strategy then there are lots of websites that have more in-depth information, and I urge you to do further research, take professional advice from a stockbroker and gain more experience in the stock market before even considering this.

Buy To Cover – If you give this order to your brokerage firm then it will buy back the shares that were sold short – remember the brokerage firm will have borrowed these on your behalf and thus will return them (usually to another brokerage firm) so that the short position is covered.

Okay, so those are the basic ways an order can be marked. Now we shall look at the different order types.

Market Order

This has the name of the company whose shares you are purchasing and the amount in pounds, but there is no time or specified price stated.

For example, the order might state;

'Buy £500 of Company X' or 'sell £500 of Company X'. This would mean you are either buying or selling £500 worth of shares in the company. As there is no specific price or time attached the market order it is assumed that the investor wants to either buy or sell immediately and therefore, they get the price that the shares are when the order reaches the electronic trading platform or trading floor. For a buy option, it should be the lowest possible price and for a sell option it should be the highest possible price but of course, if these prices have fluctuated by the time the order is executed the investor will get whatever the market price is at this point.

Instead of 'buy' and 'sell' you may see the terms 'invest' or 'raise' which mean the same thing. For the purpose of this book, I will continue to use 'buy' and 'sell' because I think these are the terms that people understand and tend to associate with the stock market.

Limit Order

This is where an investor has a specific price they want to buy or sell at.

For example, it might be to sell £500 of Company X at 1150p or buy £500 of Company X at 700p.

Note that the share price is given in pence not pounds.

This order will only be carried out when the market price reaches that which the investor has specified or is better than that which is specified.

So why would we use a buy limit order? Why would we not just buy shares immediately?

To answer this, let's look at two scenarios.

Firstly, let's pretend you want to purchase shares in Company X. You want the best possible price and therefore would like to buy when the shares are low, hoping that an increase will soon be on the cards. Let's say Company X has a share price of 800p. They have currently dropped to 700p, but you believe that very soon they are going to decrease further before picking up again. Therefore, you don't want to pay the 700p; you want to wait for them to drop to 660p and so you place a *buy* limit order for this.

If the price rises, then your order will be cancelled by the end of the day because it is lower than the current market price. If the price continues to decrease, however, then your order will be placed. Of course, the point of buying them at a low price is because you anticipate many other investors doing the same which will, in turn, cause the price to rise again. The risk you take here, therefore, is that the price could continue to decline after the limit order has gone through which means you end up with stocks that are worth less than what you paid for even at the buy limit order price. Had you hung on a little bit longer then you may have got a better deal, the worst-case scenario, however, is that you end up with shares that never regain the higher price you were hoping for.

The other side of this coin, of course, will be if the shares don't reach the price you anticipated. Let's say they reached 665p and then started to rise; your buy limit order won't be executed, and therefore you will miss out on the shares altogether.

You could also have a buy to cover limit order to buy back shares that have been sold short. Let's say you had sold short shares in Company X when the price was 900p. The current market price now is 800p, but you anticipate they are going to drop further than this. You place a buy to cover limit order in at 660p. If the prices drop to this, then the order will be acted upon; you will make a tidy profit and the shares will be returned.

Again, the risk here is that the shares don't drop to the price you have chosen but start to rise before they reach this; best-case scenario here would be that you would begin to lose some of your profit, worst-case scenario is they rise too quick for you to sell and you end up paying more to buy them back than you sold them for.

Let's now look at a sell limit order.

In this scenario, you, as an investor, owns shares in Company X. They are currently at 1150p but you think they are going to decline quickly in the foreseeable future. You place a limit order to sell your shares at 1190p; *above* the current market price. This is because you believe the share price will creep up before it drops and you will, therefore, get the best possible price for your shares.

If the market price continues to rise your order will be executed at the 1190p mark...however the risk you take is that the shares drop before they reach this price in which case your sell limit order will be cancelled...in this scenario, you could end up holding shares that have declined dramatically in price.

Let's look at this same scenario again but this time you are selling short shares in Company X: remember when you sell short, you are selling borrowed shares which you will have to buy back at some point. You think that the price will decline so put the sell limit order in at 1190p; the price rises and your order is fulfilled. Should the price now decline after this you will buy back the shares for the lower price and will have made a nice profit.

The risk here is that the price doesn't decline but continues to rise after your sell limit order has been carried out as you could end up having to buy them back at a higher price.

Summary

Just to summarise as this is can seem complicated; a buy limit order is placed *below* the current market price and is used to buy into the market to take advantage of a temporary dip before an anticipated rise.

A sell limit order is placed *above* current market price and is used to sell your shares (liquidate your position) or sell short at a higher price in anticipation of a sharp decline in the near future. Remember unless the share price reaches that which you specified your order will not be acted upon.

Marketable Limit Order

This is a variation of the limit order described above, but rather than being placed above or below the current market price, it is entered at the current price a share is trading.

Let's say you want to buy Company Y shares for 700p which is the current market price. You put in a marketable limit order for this price.

Wait; I hear you asking, isn't this the same as a market order? It has no time attached so is therefore executed immediately, right?

True but with one small difference; with a market order, you don't set a time, therefore, you get the price the share is at when your order reaches the trading floor or the electronic trading platform as the case is likely to be these days. By the time your order is carried out, the price could have rocketed way above this. If this is the case then the marketable limit order won't be acted upon and your shares won't be purchased. If the shares dropped however then you would get them at this new, lower price.

With a marketable limit order to sell, you would specify the current market price and therefore your shares would only be sold at this price or higher. Consequently, you may gain money if the price is higher by the time your order is fulfilled but if not you at least know you won't be selling for less than your specified price.

Summary

A mini summary to emphasise the difference between a market order and a marketable limit order.

With a market order, your order is acted upon immediately but as you haven't specified the price by the time it is fulfilled the market price could have increased or decreased which means you could end up paying more (or selling for less) than you wanted to.

With a marketable limit order, you have the reassurance that your shares will be bought (or sold) at the price you specified or better.

Stop Order (Stop Loss Order)

For this order you must specify a price, known as the stop price; when the share price reaches this level, the order is changed into a market order. A stop order is used by those investors who want to limit their losses or protect any profits they may have made by selling short.

Let's look at a scenario; you've bought company X shares that are currently trading at 700p. You are worried that these shares might decline unexpectedly, which means you would make a loss; therefore, you decide to set a sell stop order at, let's say, 680p. Unless the shares drop to this price, the order won't be executed. However, clearly, if the price drops and the stop order is set in motion you will make a loss because it is lower than the price you paid. In this example, you will lose *at least* 20p per share BUT if you didn't place this sell stop order and the share price went into free fall then you could lose a lot more.

Now, you may have noticed you I said '*at least*' this amount will be lost; that's because you could lose more by the time the order is carried out because when the price reaches the stop price the order is changed into a market order. The price you get isn't the stop price (although it could be if you're lucky) but the current market price at the time the order is carried out. Therefore, if the share continues to fall then it could be a lot lower by the time it reaches the trading floor (or acted upon by the trading platform).

Remember a stop order limits your losses; it doesn't protect against them.

Another way to use a sell stop order is to protect any

profit you may make if your shares rise. Placing an order below the normal volatility of the market will protect some of your profit. This is sometimes known as a trailing stop-loss order.

In this scenario it is important to keep in mind the phrase 'normal volatility'; remember the market is volatile at the best of times and prices can go up and down by the second. If you place your stop price too close to normal market price it could be triggered, and you could then find that you have sold your shares and two minutes later the price has risen again. Unfortunately, I can't say place a stop order at X amount or even recommend a percentage because all shares are different and the market is continually changing. All I can say is that you – or your stockbroker – have to determine what is normal market volatility and what would be the shares going into free fall.

A more practical way to look at it is to ask yourself how much are you willing to lose? Or how much do you want to protect? For example, if you can afford to – or are happy to – lose, say, five per cent of your profit then you would set it five per cent below what you paid for the shares or if you are working in pence then if you are happy to lose, say, 30p per share then you set your stop price 30p below what you paid for it.

A buy stop order, again, is used to limit high losses or protect profit if you sell short.

Let's look at another scenario; this time you believe a company's shares are about to decline. You sell short at 760p. Now I mentioned earlier that the issue with selling short is that if the market price increases you could end up paying more than you sold the shares for. Therefore, to protect some of your potential profit – or at least limit your losses – you can use a buy stop order. In this scenario, you would enter the order *higher* than the current market price therefore if the price increases unexpectedly the buy stop order is triggered, changed into a market order and acted upon. Like a sell stop order, the price you set is only the trigger; what you end up paying will be whatever the current market price is when the order is acted upon.

If a short position becomes profitable; that is if you sell short and the price declines – let's say you sold at 750p per share and the price drops to 700p per share – you may want to protect this profit. To do this you can set a buy stop order just above the current market price; if the price moves lower you can adjust the buy stop order – this is known as a trailing stop-loss order.

Stop Limit Order

This is similar to the previous order but as well as specifying a stop price, you – the investor – will also set a limit price too.

On a sell stop limit the limit price is the same or lower than the stop price whereas with a buy stop limit order the limit price is the same or higher than the stop price.

It is a more cautious version of a stop order because with a stop order the price is the trigger to change the order to a market order which means the share is bought or sold at whatever the current market price is when the order is carried out. With a stop-limit order your order is changed to a marketable limit order and therefore you will get the price you specified or better.

Trading Strategies

Educate Yourself

This book is a great starting point, but I cannot possibly cover everything you need to know here, if I did it would be the size of an encyclopaedia. Choose your companies and then research them but also look for advice from people who are out there trading themselves. There are plenty of people out there who are willing to give out advice and share their stories. Whilst I am hesitant to give out any specific recommendations on companies because they change so much that by the time you read this the recommendations may have changed, many of these gurus will also recommend particular stocks and shares or companies that are doing really well and are investable at the moment.

Whilst I'd never recommend that you buy and sell just because someone on YouTube told you to, I do think that following a few of these experts will help you learn good strategies and give you an idea of what to look for in your own stocks. The more you can learn, the better your decisions and the more likely you are that you will make more return on your investments.

There are also some brilliant apps out there for investors just starting out in the stock market, and some of these are in essence tools that can help you learn about shares and how to trade.

Choose A trade Market Based On Your Budget And Trading Style

While I would always advocate that you play it safe as a beginner, I haven't met you and I don't know how confident you are nor how willing you are to take risks. I can't, in good faith, say "go out there and invest £10,000 in the stock market in this, this and this" because I don't have a crystal ball and can't see how investments are going to play out in the future nor do I know what your personality is like and how happy you are to lose the money you invest.

Research each market thoroughly and understand what the pros and cons are and what each market can offer you. For example. Forex investing tends to have the smallest minimum investment amount yet can give you quick returns. Trading futures can cost high amounts and take longer to provide you with any decent returns.

Another consideration is your time zone; if you pick a

foreign market you may find that you are up at 3am to check on your investments. This, of course, doesn't work if you are also raising a family and/or holding down a full-time job.

Finally, your trading style will play a part; if you are willing to take risks, then you may decide that one you have a handle on the stock market that penny stocks are a gamble you are willing to take or you may invest and decide that it's too much work and stress and therefore change your mind about investing as an individual and decide to enter into a fund instead.

When Should I Sell My Shares?

The answer to this, in an ideal world, should be "when they are at their highest peak" but of course, we aren't living in an ideal world; you are not going to buy stocks, hold on to them for twenty years, watch the share price steadily increase and then sell them making a million-pound profit.

Selling shares at the wrong time can lead to poor portfolio performance and can reduce the amount of returns you end up with overall; therefore it is good to know when to sell your stocks.

To Limit Losses

My recommendation to those new to the stock market is to invest for the long term and hold on to shares, but sometimes this won't always work in your favour. If you just bury your head in the sand you could end up with shares that aren't worth anywhere near what you first paid for them and whilst, if you are in it for the long haul, markets can change in your favour, sometimes it is clear that you should get out and move on to something else. Sometimes you just need to cut your losses and rather than being seen as a failed attempt should be seen as a positive move whenever you feel uncertain about the future of particular shares.

Sometimes you may need to admit that you've made a mistake, for example, if you read the trends wrong or you invested in an industry that you thought would boom but actually is showing signs of slowing down or declining. If you feel like you've made a mistake, then you should look again at your investments, do a bit more research and garner some advice in order to decide whether it makes sense to keep hold of these investments or to sell and move on to something else.

To Take A Profit

Selling shares is how you make a profit in the long term and there is going to be a time when you need to sell shares in order to gain the cash that is tied up in these investments. Choosing when to do this can be difficult and there is no 'one fits all' type of answer because it depends on your strategy and attitude to trading. My advice is to hold on to profitable shares for as long as you can unless there is something that suggests you should sell at this time.

When The Future Is Pessimistic

As much as we'd all love to be optimistic all of the time, the truth is sometimes markets start to decline and share prices can show a downward trend. One contributing factor to this is that investors are pessimistic about the prospects in that particular market or that particular company. There are various reasons for this pessimism which we will look at later on but if you see news that signals a pessimistic market you should sell quickly because chances are other traders are all going to do the same which will cause the share price to drop. Markets tend to move in herds so when there is bad news looming it is usually safe to assume that people are soon going to be selling their shares and therefore to maximise your profits and minimise your loss you should seriously consider selling before everyone else follows suit.

If The Price Reaches Your Target

It is often wise to set sell targets so you are protected if a price drops or rises. Decide what you can afford to lose. For instance, if you decide you can live with a 20% loss on an investment then have this as your limit so if a share price drops by 20% then you will sell this regardless of the circumstances. This may seem a bit silly as you could wait a bit longer until the price rises again, right? Yes, you could but what happens if they continue to fall and you end up losing 50% of your investment or even the whole lot if the company is in financial trouble and ends up going into administration? Likewise, you can set sell targets for price rises in order to protect your profit. This does mean you may miss out if you end up investing in a company that turns out to be the next Apple or Amazon and the price triples in value but the odds of this happening are slim and if you are happy with a 20% increase then it is wise that you take your profits and run so to speak before the share prices shift back to the initial price you paid or lower.

If The Market Reverses

It is important that you check the market and economic trends of shares because it is advisable to sell at the sign of a market reversal. As a newbie, you might not be confident at recognising when a market is going to go into reversal so you could wait a little while until it is definitely showing a decline in prices. This would cost you some money but it is often better than just selling every time there's a slight dip and it will allow you to learn the signals of a downward spiral. Really investing in the stock market can often be a case of trial and error; the trick is to not ignore market reversals so long that you end up losing more money than you need to.

Company Changes

It is important to remember why you chose the specific companies you invested in? It shouldn't just be to make a profit but because you believe in the company and the industry it operates in or because you have an interest in what they do or maybe you liked their ethos. Whatever it was, if the companies you invested in change then you should start to consider selling your shares. These changes could be to do with the amount of debt that a company is taking on or because of a change in the balance sheet, a change in management or any other actions that alter the way it operates. If the company you invested in is shifting away from what it used to be when you originally invested and the reason you invested isn't there now then you should carefully consider whether you want to be a part of them anymore.

Another thing to keep an eye on is dividends and how the company pay them. If they have started to pay out more of their profits, whilst this may give you an increase in money for a year or two, it could actually be a sign that the company is having difficulty growing. On the other hand, if a company that used to pay out a lot of profits in dividends but has suddenly reduced this and has reinvested more into the company then it could be a sign that it is changing the way that it operates.

Rapid Price Changes

This could be rapid increases or rapid decreases and both are signals to reconsider your investments. If a company's share price rises too quickly it could be that it's been wrongly valued by the market, it's gained new business that has a significant impact on its share price or some insider knowledge has been leaked leading people to believe it is a good investment. It may seem great that this share price has increased if you have some – and it is – but it could also mean a sudden decline which is why it is sensible to set a sell target and get out while the going is good.

Likewise, if a share price suddenly starts to rapidly decline then you should sell in order to avoid making too much of a loss.

Re-Evaluating

It is important to monitor your investments so that you don't miss out on signs that you should have sold. However, it doesn't mean you have to immediately panic sell just because you have noticed a potential sell scenario; you just need to consider whether it is worthwhile, are there signs that the share price is going to rise again or is it clearly in free fall? It also comes down to the risk you are willing to take; you may decide that you are going to gamble and just watch the stock market to see what happens or you may decide that you don't want to risk any more money and therefore selling is the best option. It really comes down to doing more research and increasing your knowledge in order to become more confident with your decisions and improve the way you invest. I would always say if in doubt don't change your strategy but if you are really in doubt then take advice from someone experienced and more knowledgeable than yourself.

One thing to be aware of is stock market crashes such as the stock market crash of Oct. 29, 1929. This crash marked the start of the Great Depression and sparked America's most famous bear market. The S&P 500 fell 86 per cent in less than three years and did not regain its previous peak until 1954. If there is ever talk about similar happening, you should always seek independent advice, and approach new investments with extreme caution.

Chapter 7:
Diversifying

Know The Risks

Let's say you had a £15,000 inheritance and you decided to invest it in the stock market. People keep telling you about this great technology company whose products are popular, the company is fast-growing and share prices are low but are expected to increase. It sounds great, right? You decide to invest all your inheritance in this company because you can and because this will give you more shares thus resulting in higher dividends should the company decide to pay these. Everything is great, the share prices increase and you get a high dividend in year one. However, the next year things start to crumble; the products become too highly-priced and customers aren't willing to buy them. Bad news circulates amongst the media about the company's financial situation and its future growth prospects. Shareholders become nervous and they start to sell their shares but people don't want to buy them because they've heard the bad news and want to make sure that the shares stabilise before they purchase and so the share price plummets. What was worth £15,000 last year is now only worth £10,000.

The above is a simple example and is possibly not very likely although there were some issues like this in real-life with the technology companies and the so-called dot com craze but what it illustrates is that should you invest purely in one company and for whatever reason, it gets into financial difficulty and the share prices drop then you could lose all your money. With this example, you would have lost £5,000, a third of your investment. Had you invested, say, £6,000 and lost a third of your investment, the loss would only have been £2,000, significantly lower and the other £7,000 would have been in other investments earning you dividends or increasing in share price.

Company Risk

What the above example is showing is company-specific risk, also known as unsystematic risk. Investing in a company is risky because nobody can predict how that company is going to perform year on year. A company-specific risk only impacts one company.

Sector Risk

When a risk affects all the companies in a specific sector it is called sector risk so using the example above if the bad news that had been circulating hadn't been about the company you had invested in specifically, but about the sector as a whole, it could result in people selling shares across the whole sector. For this reason, it is not advised that you put all your money into different companies within the same sector.

Market Risk

Market risk – or systematic risk – refers to a decline in the investment markets as a whole rather than one specific sector. For example, during August and September 2011 there were wild fluctuations in all stocks and therefore no matter how you had diversified, should you have had all your money in stocks and shares then for this period of time your whole portfolio would have declined in value on certain days.

What can you do to alleviate market risk? Other than either anticipating a decline and trying to sell before it happens or holding onto the shares and hoping and praying fervently that they will start to go up again then not much.

There is a sophisticated strategy that involves derivatives such as index options and futures to hedge against this sort of portfolio value decline, but these hedging strategies are incredibly complex and require more specific types of information and skills that are going far beyond the scope of this book which is intended for beginners.

As this book is aimed at those who are new to the stock market then these tips on how to set up a diverse portfolio are enough for now and should see that your investments are as secure as they can be and should mean that you see some return on your investment. Once you become more confident and familiar with the stock markets, then you can start to find out more about hedging and other, more complicated strategies.

How To Diversify

Okay, when I say 'portfolio' I'm really just referring to the number of stocks and shares you hold. 'Diversifying your portfolio' is just a posher way of saying 'don't put all your eggs in one basket'. Basically, when you are holding investments – whether it is stocks and shares or any other type of investment – you really don't want to put all your money into the exact same thing as shown in the example at the beginning of this chapter.

So how do you diversify your portfolio?

Have Different Investments

Make sure your portfolio has many different investments. As well as investing in an individual company also consider investing in Bonds, Exchange-Traded Funds, Mutual funds and Index funds

The reasoning behind this is that the value of these different assets will be affected by different things. For example, bonds tend to be influenced the most by interest rates. Property values, whilst also susceptible to interest rates, tend to be affected by how well the domestic economy is performing. Shares tend to change depending on how well a company performs. Therefore, if you have money in, say, shares and bonds and the companies in your portfolio decline due to a media story, your bonds shouldn't be affected therefore your portfolio overall should remain healthy.

Don't Stick To One Company

I've mentioned this already but just to reiterate if you buy lots of shares in one company then it is higher risk than if you split your investments across many companies because if this company goes bust then all your money goes with it.

Diversify By Sector

Just like you shouldn't buy all your shares in just one company, you shouldn't invest in just one sector either.

Hindsight is a wonderful thing, and there are a few times we can look back on now and use as examples of what not to do. For instance, the dot com bubble of 2000-2002 when everybody invested in the tech sector and companies that had barely made any secure business plans suddenly went public and people invested in them. Millionaires were made overnight but then the market crashed and others ended up with shares that were completely useless. Another example of not putting all your money in one sector is the credit crunch of 2007. If you had shares in a bank in the UK in 2006 you would have been doing very well, and many people were. This encouraged them to buy more shares but they diversified by buying into different banks thinking that this made them secure. However suddenly the banking crisis hit and share prices plummeted. What seemed like a diversified portfolio really wasn't because this crisis affected the whole sector not just one or two individual companies.

To be completely diverse you need to find assets that are not closely related, so if you were to invest in the health care sector, you would then also want to find another company in a completely different sector such as food and beverages or manufacturing.

Look At Different Geographical Regions

I did say earlier that I don't recommend you venturing into foreign exchange markets right now as a newcomer to the stock market, but that doesn't mean you shouldn't do it at all. Once you get the hang of picking stocks and shares then you can think about doing this as spreading your investments across the globe can mean that you protect yourself against certain influences such as the economic conditions of a country or a government's economic policies. For example, if the UK stock market performs badly it doesn't necessarily affect the stock market of China. However, I don't advise you delve straight into international markets because these can bring their own risks with them; for example, Brazil, India, Russia and China are all fairly volatile and are classed as emerging markets whereas the UK and USA are developed markets and therefore less volatile. One thing you can do is look at the FTSE 100 and invest in some international markets listed on there as they tend to be more stable.

Word Of Warning

Okay, this may seem contradictory as I've just spent this whole chapter telling you to diversify, buy shares in lots of different companies, in different sectors, in different geographical areas and markets and now I'm going to say don't OVER diversify. There is a difference and yes, you can over diversify if you get overly excited and decide that you want to buy, buy, buy and spread your investments too thinly.

You might not be putting your investments at risk in so far as you end up losing money, but you could hold yourself back if you so little money in each investment that you don't see much in the way of returns.

Usually the rule of thumb is don't have more than twenty to thirty investments in total whether this be shares or bonds or (hopefully) a mixture of the two. This way you should be putting a good proportion of your money in each investment so as to see positive results.

What Should I Invest In?

So you now know that you should invest in different assets to be truly diverse but as this book is looking at the stock market we are going to just be looking at the proportion you choose to invest in shares and forget about the rest so when I talk about investments in this section I am only referring to your share portfolio.

If you want a relatively safe portfolio then you would be wise to invest your money in bonds, UK equities and US equities.

If you wanted to be riskier then a smaller proportion of your investments would be in UK equities and more would be in more volatile, emerging markets. Another way of dividing up your share portfolio would be by investing in low risk, blue-chip companies and high-risk smaller companies. If you want to be low risk and play it safe then the majority of your shares would be in these blue-chip companies, preferably ones that pay dividends.

There is nothing wrong with this strategy BUT if you really want to see high returns on your investments then you are going to have to take risks. This would mean having a higher percentage of your money in smaller, more volatile companies and less in blue-chip, safer companies. Smaller companies tend to have quicker growth whereas the bigger companies are often just steadily plodding along. Of course, these smaller companies that would bring in the higher returns may not be ones you have heard of before and it is a risk because there may not be enough data to show whether they are sustainable or not or whether anyone else wants to invest in them.

Changing Your Portfolio

You will need to assess your portfolio regularly and you may need to rebalance it now and then. I would suggest you do this on an annual basis because as tempting as it can be to tinker with your portfolio after three months or six months, try to resist this otherwise you could end up losing out on potential for growth.

The only time it is necessary to change your portfolio is either if you have a stock that is clearly not doing well and the company is in real difficulty making it clear that these shares are not going to increase in value or if your investments don't marry up with your original plan. For example, if one equity grows more quickly than another. For instance, let's say you have 70% of your equities in the UK, 20% in the US markets and the other 10% in an emerging market, say, China. If your equities in China grow to, say 30% of your portfolio and your UK market drops to, say 50% of your portfolio you may want to minimise your risk by rebalancing this which would mean selling some of the shares you hold in Chinese companies and investing this money into the UK market.

Beginner Portfolio

It is easy to get to get carried away about making investments as the stock market can be very exciting; especially when you see your shares increasing in price. I wouldn't recommend that you just jump in with both feet without dipping your toe into the water first though. By this, I mean that rather than investing in the stock market immediately you should set up a beginner portfolio and start share watching before you part with your money.

There are some websites and apps that allow you to

set up a beginner – or virtual – portfolio but sometimes they don't allow you to do this unless you commit to opening an account first. I would check the small print thoroughly before you commit to anything; don't set up an account just because they have an app, you want to make sure they meet other requirements too in order to help your success in the stock market.

So, what is a beginner portfolio?

Basically, it's just like a real portfolio only you are just watching the shares instead of actually investing in them.

To get started I would advise you pick one or two companies you are interested in investing in. Do your research and if you think they are sound investments then think about how much money you would realistically invest in them.

Pretend you have bought these shares; you could set up a spreadsheet with the number of shares you would potentially buy and the amount of money it would cost you and then start watching these shares. Set yourself a time period over which to watch these shares. You can be researching other companies during this time. Each time you decide you would like to invest in a company you have researched, add it to your beginner portfolio spreadsheet. Let's say, you give yourself two weeks or a month, check the shares at different times of the day and see how they are doing; make a note of it on your spreadsheet. At the end of the time period look at how much the shares are now worth and whether you would have made money or not.

Don't forget to take into account any potential charges you would have incurred had you invested in the stock market for real such as trading costs, stamp duty and so on, and deduct these from your total.

Okay, I think you may be asking, why? What is the point of setting up a beginner portfolio? What if my shares were cheap at the time I considered purchasing them and then the price goes through the roof? Not only will I have to pay more for them, but I may have missed out on an amazing opportunity?

This can happen, I'm not going to lie, but it doesn't happen very often. The beginner portfolio is great because it gives you the opportunity to choose shares and watch the stock market without losing any money. It allows you to see how it works before you start investing.

By monitoring the shares of the companies you are interested in it gives you the chance to see how good you are at choosing shares; on your first time you may research a company but not pick up on valuable bits of information or you may misinterpret something, if the share price plummets then you could end up losing money if you had invested straight away but setting up a beginner portfolio means you can see whether you have a knack for choosing stocks or if you need a little bit more help. This means you may end up not investing in some companies you had originally chosen and it can also help you decide whether you want to set up a stocks and shares account entirely on your own or whether you want to re-think this and use either a Robo-Advisor, join a fund or use a financial advisor or a full stockbroker service instead.

By building up a portfolio before investing means that you may have two or three companies at the end of your set time period that you feel are sound investments. This means, if you have the money available, you could invest in these companies at once, thus, in theory, avoiding extra potential trading charges that you may incur had you just bought a few shares one month and a few shares the next.

Finally, setting up a virtual portfolio instead of a real one gives you time to see how you react personally to the stock market and any potential gains or losses. If you stress out or feel ill every time one of your potential company's has a dip in the share price then you may decide that investing isn't for you.

To some people, setting up a beginner portfolio may seem a bit wishy-washy and if you are a risk-taker with money to spare you may decide to skip this step and this is entirely up to you. However, if you are new to the stock market and are a bit uncertain then I think it is important to set up a portfolio whilst you are still in the research stage.

Chapter 8:

Analysing the Market

There are two ways to analyse the markets; one is fundamental analysis and the other is technical analysis.

A technical analyst will look at charts and patterns of past price and volume movement to decide whether an individual stock or the market as a whole is likely to rise or decline in the future.

A fundamental analyst, on the other hand, will take a holistic approach to the markets and look at a variety of factors before making any investment decisions. For example, micro-economic factors such as costs of production, labour, supply and demand or macro-economic factors such as the sectors that are thriving in that economy as a whole, the health of the entire country's economy, how competitive a particular market is, any news reports as well as political factors.

Fundamental analysis can be applied to any markets including commodities and Forex but predominantly for the purposes of this book we will look at how they are used in relation to shares

Why Is Analysis Important?

Any sort of analysis before investing is important because otherwise, you are just investing on a whim without really knowing the ins and outs of it or what you are getting yourself into. What is the point in investing in something if you don't even know if the company – or the sector it operates in – is doing well?

Analysis can be daunting and this is a reason why many people skip it but the actual understanding is often easier than the complicated jargon and acronyms would suggest so to learn the basics can be simpler than memorising the technical terms.

Fundamental Analysis

Fundamental analysis is important because it can help you assess the intrinsic value of a company and gives you an idea of whether it is under or over-valued which in turn can help traders find entry and exit points in an investment.

When we talk about 'intrinsic' value we aren't talking about its current market value but it's 'actual' value; for instance, the current market value could be quite high but that doesn't mean this is the true worth of the company because the stock could have been overpriced and thus may end up decreasing rapidly in the future. Likewise, it may have been undervalued which shows that if somebody were to invest early, they could end up with a large profit once the market value has increased to reflect the company's true worth.

So, what should you look for? The following forms the basis of fundamental analysis. I would still recommend that you go and do further research as the more knowledge you have the better placed you will be to understand and be successful in the stock market. However, for a beginner's guide to the stock market which this book is, I believe this list will give you a good starting point into understanding the type of information you would need to research before investing any money.

Company Accounts

It is wise to check the accounts of the company which you are considering purchasing shares in as these will give you an idea of whether the company is in a good financial position or not; there is no point investing in a company whose accounts are not stable or who is not making a profit. Check to see if profit has increased year on year or if it has remained steady; these are the types of companies you want to invest in. If a company has had a steady decline in profit over the years then you may want to steer clear as it could be an indicator that it is not performing well enough to give you any sort of financial gain.

Earnings Per Share (EPS)
Investors make buying or selling decisions based on the anticipated growth of current and future

earnings and EPS is considered to be an indicator of how profitable a company is. It is calculated by dividing a company's profit by the outstanding shares of its common stock. You shouldn't have to work out the EPS because it should be reported in its financial accounts. The higher a company's EPS is, the more profitable it is thought to be. It is an important figure because it shows how much money a company makes for each share therefore a higher EPS means investors will be willing to pay more because the company has higher profits.

We could now get to the jargon of primary EPS, fully diluted EPS or Earnings Before Interest, Taxes, Depreciation and Amortisation (EBITDA) but I imagine your eyes are already glazing over and I don't think it is necessary to unpick all these terms at this stage as a beginner investor. However, I do recommend that you try to learn about these later on if you continue your journey into the stock market and decide to invest more.

What is important to know at this stage is that EPS can be simply smoke and mirrors if the company is clever with its accounts; for example, an increased EPS can be due to the company buying its own stock back, therefore, you should look at the EPS in relation to the EPS of other organisations in the same industry; if some have a higher EPS than others in the same industry then you should be able to find a plausible explanation as to why this is.

Look at the income statement as well so that you fully understand the expenses of the company and how it's managed, for instance, net margins, operating margins and gross margin are all good for evaluating expenses. You should also look at the cash flow statement and operating cash flow statement per share in comparison to the EPS; ideally, the operating cash flow per share should be higher than the EPS. A red flag would be if the operating cash flow is negative or hasn't increased yet the EPS has grown then this would need deeper analysis.

There are many expert analysts out there who will try and predict a company's EPS and whether it will increase or decrease and these predictions, whilst

STOCK MARKET INVESTING FOR BEGINNERS

good for you as an investor to keep an eye on, can affect the share price both prior to the anticipated EPS announcement and on the day it is made public because if earnings exceed expectations and analysts have stated that they believe this to continue, more investors will try to purchase the shares. If the EPS is lower than the analyst's expectations however, investors may try to sell which can, in turn, cause the price to drop drastically. As an investor, you should check the EPS, listen to the analysts and if you are confident that the share price is going to continue to increase, try to buy shares before the EPS announcement in anticipation of other people deciding to do the same thing.

Generally, a decrease in EPS is a negative indicator because it can mean lower turnover and/or higher costs which in turn leads to lower profits IN THEORY. There are other factors that can cause this EPS to reduce. For example, conditions in a particular sector or the overall economy could mean all businesses are affected and this could just be a particular phase in the business cycle that you could ride out if you have invested long term.

Internally there could be a stock split or a payment of a stock dividend instead of a cash one; these are generally seen as positive developments especially if there is no decrease in total earnings of ordinary shares BUT it will negatively affect the EPS because there will be an increase in the number of ordinary shares outstanding.

For these reasons EPS shouldn't be the only thing you look at.

PE Ratio
When you do any sort of research into the stock market you will most likely come across the PE ratio which is the price/earnings ratio. In simple terms, it shows an investor how a company's share price fares in comparison to its earnings. To work it out you simply divide the current market price by the earnings per share.

For analysis purposes, you should compare current PE ratios to past ones for the company you are investing in as well as comparing them to other companies in the same sector and the market overall measured by a broad market index such as the FTSE

100. There are lots of investment analysis and information websites or stockbroker websites that have this information.

Keep in mind that a company that is just starting out may not have any earnings just yet and therefore, in theory, shouldn't have a PE ratio. Therefore if you come across a young company that has a high PE ratio this could indicate it is in an emerging or aggressive growth industry; investors are willing to pay a high market price despite there not being any earnings just yet because they are optimistic about the future growth potential of the company and are expecting its earnings to be high.

If a more established company has a high PE ratio in comparison to others in the sector then this could signal that they have been overvalued and thus share prices are likely to drop very soon.

What does this mean for a new investor?
Well a low PE ratio is characteristic of companies in mature, slow-growth industries such as utilities, pharmaceuticals or supermarket chains. Many blue-chip companies have low PE ratios but continue to

have high earnings consistently.

Some people, therefore, view the PE ratio as a stable investment but others believe that the shares are too low and have been undervalued. For someone who has the latter view then they would purchase shares and wait for them to be fairly valued and thus rise in price. I would only recommend this if you have extra research which supports this view.

Analysts also look at the collective PE ratios of all stocks on the FTSE 100 index; if the overall PE ratio is low then this could indicate the market is reaching its bottom and a rally may occur. If the overall PE ratio is too high then this could indicate the market is reaching its peak and will soon decline.

Therefore, if you owned shares in the above situations you would either buy and wait for the market to rally or you would sell before the prices declined.

Whichever way you interpret it, a high PE ratio is generally an indicator of higher volatility and risk and therefore, you need to weigh up carefully whether you want to take this extra risk or not.

My advice for new investors is to look for a PE ratio of no more than five or six (this means shares are trading at a price five or six times the company's earnings)

Qualitative Analysis

Fundamental Analysis can also be qualitative as in it can't be measured or quantified in mathematical figures. This can be seen as more subjective which is why some people disregard fundamental analysis in favour of more technical types but it is important as it can affect the company.

An example of qualitative fundamental analysis would be knowing the business and the quality of its management. Something I have mentioned previously in this book is never to invest in what you don't understand and knowing the business means understanding what the company does and how it makes money in a way that is simple; I would always say, can you explain it in a way that others will understand? If you can't then you don't know fully what you are investing in.

We sometimes also disregard people who work for the company yet these are often integral to the company and are what steer it in the right direction and help it get through tough times. Research the company and try to get an idea of its management; for example, have the people who hold significant roles in the company been successful elsewhere? Do they have the right experience and knowledge to make it work? Degrees and other qualifications are all very well and good, but these don't necessarily prove that someone can be successful and implement a long-term plan that sends the company onto a successful path that will last long into the future. Also, try to get an idea of what employees think to the management and the company? Does the company have a high turnover? If so, this could signal that employees aren't happy and leave which in turn can have an effect on how the company operates.

Is the company viewed favourably by the public? If there's always negative media or poor feedback about a company, it's ethics or its products then chances are the stock price will fall as people won't want to be associated with it or will worry about its future.

To summarise, fundamental analysis looks at the wider picture of a company. It looks at company accounts as well as human leadership because this can all affect the stock market price.

Fundamental analysis, however, is seen as being more suited to the long-term investor rather than the short term one because it can take a while for these types of factors to affect the price of a stock.

My advice is to use it in conjunction with technical analysis in order to gain as complete a picture about the companies you are investing in as possible.

Chapter 9:
Common Mistakes

As I keep reiterating; investing in the stock market is NOT a guaranteed return on your money but you should make some money eventually. However, there are some common mistakes that those new to the stock market make.

Mistake #1: Thinking It's Quick And Easy

Why are you investing in shares? Answer this question honestly, is it because you like the company you are investing in or is it because you think it's a good way to make some easy money? Social media has a lot to answer for in that people hear so many stories about those who have made thousands and thousands of pounds in the stock market, and they make it sound easy so we all think 'I could do that!"

Let me tell you now; it's not quick and it's not easy! You need to put in your research. Yes, there are people that buy stocks, wait a few days and sell them for a profit but is it quick and easy? No! Because they don't just buy a few random stocks; they do research, and they look for things like technical analysis and fundamental analysis, they look at the number of shares issued and they keep a close eye on their stocks so that they know when to sell. These people have been in the stock markets for a while and they most likely have lost money as well as made it; they just don't tell you about it!

If you are looking for a quick moneymaker, stocks and shares isn't it but if you are looking to put effort into finding the shares that will bring you long term gains and are willing to build up a good portfolio then you should do well in the stock market.

Mistake #4: Investing More Than Is Sensible

Don't invest money you can't afford to lose; if you take only one thing from this book, then please let it be this! £500 is a lot of money, to some people it means more than others but if you are investing this amount and you will be upset if you lost it all then don't invest it in stocks and shares.

My recommendation is you take a couple of hundred pounds and invest it and then don't invest any more until you have a feel for the stock market as well as a grip on your own emotions; if you are going to become stressed every time a stock goes down then you may not want to invest more money which will cause you more stress. You should always be comfortable with the amount you are investing. Keep some money to one side for that proverbial rainy day so you don't need to touch your stock market investments.

Mistake #3: Taking Stock Tips

Now I'm not saying don't take stock tips ever; you may know someone who is a professional trader who has made millions and knows exactly what they're doing in as much as anyone can know exactly what they're doing in the stock market. Take tips from that person!

However, if you take tips from a friend or neighbour or the friendly taxi driver who dropped you off at home after your night out then you may end up losing. Whilst these people might well be informed, most of the time they are not and taking a stock tip is no different to betting on a horse in the Grand National because someone told you it was a sure thing.

Also taking stock tips from big sources, like those people on late-night TV that always seem angry and in a rush as they shout 'buy this' and 'sell that', doesn't always give you an advantage. Why? Because everybody is hearing the same thing and as we know, share prices go up and down depending on supply and demand so if you're watching somebody on YouTube saying "this is my big tip of the day, buy 1000 shares in Company X" if five hundred people are watching the same thing and all go and buy 1000 shares in Company X, what will happen? The price will go up of course and then when the same YouTube person says "sell all your shares in Company X" the price will then drop if everyone acted upon it.

Take people's opinion and then do your own research. If you think the tip is good but you can invest in a similar field rather than the same company as everyone else then sometimes this is better but don't buy stocks just because millions of people are hearing the same information and doing the same thing.

Mistake #4: Becoming Emotionally Attached

I mentioned that you should invest in what you know and invest in a company because you want to own it not because you want to make money from it BUT at the end of the day you do want to make money from it so don't treat it as anything more than an investment because if you do you could end up hanging onto a stock when you should be selling it.

Mistake #5: Trading Without A Strategy

You *need* a strategy; even 'I'm buying £5000 worth of shares in 5 companies and leaving it for the next ten years' is a strategy. You need to know what you are aiming for; do you want money for retirement or do you just want to make some extra money each year from dividends? Don't just trade on a whim; build a portfolio based around your strategy whether that is to put half your money into high-risk investments that will give potentially higher returns or whether it is to put 80% of your money into low risk, low returns investments and 20% into high risk, high return ones; whatever you want to do just make a plan and stick to it.

Mistake #6: Selling At A Loss

Sometimes you have to sell shares and take the hit if you know that a company that you have invested in is in financial trouble and the shares are going to plummet but try not to panic sell. Some stocks do plummet but in the long term they tend to go up again; even in a recession when shares drop and become worthless, as long as the company is still trading eventually, historically, they have gone back up; it just takes time. For example, Sainsbury's share price reduced by around 5% in 2019 when there were talks of a merger between themselves and Asda. People started selling their shares yet this is such a big company and the price was affected because of the uncertainty around this move. Those that sold may have made a mistake because these shares will most likely increase again.

There are exceptions to the rule however and you need to determine whether it is right to hold on or whether it is better to make a loss. An example of this would be Blackberry who was doing incredibly well but then who's share price just plummeted. Had you sold those shares when they were at their highest you would have made a good profit but those who didn't sell at the right time and were reluctant to make a loss clung on to them. You need to make the call BUT don't panic sell; just because a share price has dropped five per cent doesn't mean it won't recover; you need to learn what is short term fluctuations and what is a share price plummeting beyond no return.

Mistake #7: Disregarding Charges

Many people know that you pay a fee to buy or sell shares but don't realise (or maybe just ignore) other charges such as stamp duty, inactivity fee, et cetera. They pick an online platform that has small trading fees and don't look at anything else. They then end up making a small profit, sell their shares and find that they have actually not made any money because this small profit has been eaten up in charges. Look at the trading platform you want to use carefully; check that there are no monthly or annual account fees or any other hidden costs.

Sometimes you have to pay an annual percentage on your portfolio which doesn't sound a lot when you only have a few shares at the beginning but which end up being a huge proportion if you have a decent-sized portfolio so check this before you sign up to anything.

Mistake #8: Not Reinvesting

I have heard many people say 'oh just got a £50 dividend payment' or 'oh I sold some shares today and made £300'. I nod and say 'that's great' but what I'm really thinking is 'have you spent it already?' because what I notice is that people take these payments and they buy a new outfit, or they have a weekend away which is great, and they benefit from it but had they reinvested that money they would probably have more in the long term.

Many people are short-sighted and they take the money without thinking of the future. If you sell shares at a profit, yes you've made money, but you don't have those shares anymore. If you have a dividend payment, that's great but if you reinvest you could have more shares and end up with more dividend payments in the future.

My advice is to reinvest some of the money you make from the stock market so that you have more in the long term.

Mistake #8: Thinking The Stock Market Is A Job

I have heard people say they are going to learn about the stock market and have it as their full-time job. I say, just invest and keep an eye on those investments but think of any gains as money for the future or a little bit of extra money to boost your wages. Realistically, how many people make millions of pounds (or even thousands of pounds) on one trade? If you invest correctly you could end up with a lot of money in the future, but only if you think of it as a long-term investment.

My advice is to buy more than you sell. Beginners to the stock market however always want to sell and buy, then sell some more, buy some more and they are constantly trading yet never make high returns. This is because they don't reinvest or they make losses because they don't take into account the charges that they incur for buying and selling.

Mistake #9: Not Looking At Percentages

People look at big companies like Apple, whose stock is £1000 or more then they see that this stock goes up to, like, £1050 one day and they say 'oh if I had invested, I'd have made fifty dollars in a day'. That is true but on a £1000 investment, $50 is, like, 5%. However, if you look at a share that is, say, £20 and it goes up to £25, yes it's only £5 but percentage-wise it has gone up 25%. Had you bought £1000 worth of shares in this company and you had made £5 per share you would have made far more than if you had bought the one share at £1000.

When looking at shares it's not always about the share price but the actual percentage gain so this is something you need to keep in mind when purchasing.

Mistake #10: Investing Everything In One Company

We have already covered this so I'll keep it brief but investing all your money in one company is a no-no yet is a common mistake. Someone thinks they only have £5000 and they think that they will be able to purchase more shares if they invest it in one company than if they spread it between high and low-priced stocks and yes, this is true but what happens when people start selling their shares and the share prices drop? Or if the company goes into administration? At one point, some companies were seen as a sure thing but now even those companies who at one time or another were in the FTSE 100 are going into administration or have already gone. You only have to look at the high street to see that big names such as Mothercare, Toys R Us, BHS and Woolworths who were all incredibly profitable and 'safe' have suddenly disappeared. Many other leading high street retailers that at one point would pay out high dividends are now in financial difficulty. The question is which of them will be here in five years' time?

Conclusion

By now, you should be excited about investing in the stock market because shares can be exciting as long as you are in the right frame of mind. Now that you have reached the end of this book you will hopefully be thinking about what type of investor you are and your attitude towards the stock market as well as your reasons for investing and the stage of life you are at. Are you investing to buy a new house or a car? Do you want to save for your future retirement? Whatever your plans are, these should direct how you invest and what you invest in. For instance, if you are young and want to save for your retirement in forty years' time then you will have plenty of time on your hands and will be able to afford to take bigger risks than say, someone who is only ten years' away from retirement.

Whatever your goals are, make sure you are ready to

invest for a long period of time in order to maximise your returns. If you keep buying and selling without any sort of plan you could end up losing out if you sell shares too early before they reach their peak price or if you sell shares that are giving you dividends.

Before you invest anything at all, you need to be in a good financial position, ideally without any debts other than a mortgage. This is because the markets are volatile; if you are in debt you could end up getting into more debt. The stock markets are, in essence, another form of gambling and you need to be prepared to make losses. If you can't afford to lose money then you really shouldn't be investing in it because as much as we would all like to think we are going to become millionaires, the reality is that many of us lose at one time or another. This doesn't mean that we never make any returns but just that it's not always as high as we would like it to be. Whilst the average rate of return is 10% per year, many people don't get this.

You don't need a lot of money to invest in the stock market but if you are starting with a small amount you should increase this each month or year, for instance, even something as small as £25 a month can give you a good rate of return if you invest in the right things. If you make a profit either by selling at a higher price than you have purchased shares from or by dividend payments then it would be wise to re-invest these in order to increase the assets in your portfolio and therefore increase your rate of returns.

Evaluate your attitude to risk; if you are someone that stresses about everything and feel sick at the thought of losing any money then investing in the stock market via a financial advisor or a stockbroker that provides financial information and advice may be better for you than going it alone. If you want a steer in the right direction but don't need human interaction than a Robo-Advisor may be suited to you.

Share prices fluctuate throughout the day and this is caused by a variety of reasons. Mainly the price works on a supply and demand basis; if people want a share and demand is high but not many people are selling then this creates a higher price whereas if lots of people are selling, but nobody is buying then this makes the price drop. Remember if you are selling you can only do so if somebody is willing to buy! Investor expectations, economic and political influences and the media also affect share prices.

There are lots of trading platforms to choose from nowadays, and people are far trading online far more than they are using traditional stockbrokers. Therefore you have a lot to choose from. Do your research first to choose one that is most suited to you and your circumstances. Remember that there are lots of charges you could incur with trading so make sure you check before you sign up to anything. You may prefer to choose a platform based on the cost of buying and selling and look for one that has lower charges or you may wish to pay higher charges in return for somebody to give you some advice.

When choosing shares look at the price as this could determine what you can afford to invest in. For example, you may want to invest in Coca-Cola but if you only have £50 then you may not be able to afford more than one share, and so it may be wise to purchase something less pricey or else to wait until you can afford the shares you want.

Other considerations to take into account when choosing shares are whether you get any dividends, the EPS, market cap, revenue growth and the proven track record of a company. It is wise to find companies that have a good unique selling point that can't easily be replicated; for example, Coca-Cola is a great company to invest in because they tend to do well even in economic downturns and they have a product that is very hard for others to imitate which is why it has such a high market cap. Do your research and check analyst reports to get an insight into the companies you are interested in. Try to invest in companies and industries where you have some knowledge; either because you have used the products or because you have an interest in them. If you don't understand what a company does then it is not a viable investment because you won't know how to determine if they are doing well or not.

Diversify your portfolio by having different investments as well as stocks and shares and also having a diverse portfolio with regards to the shares you hold. For example, don't hold shares all in one company but invest in a variety, try to diversify by geographical locations and industry.

1. Investing all your money in one company is risky; if it gets into financial trouble or goes under, then your investment is lost. If you invest in numerous companies and one of them folds then you have only lost a small percentage of your overall investment.

Follow the golden rules which are:

The greater the return, the greater the risk.

If you are not willing to take risks then don't invest.

Take more risk when you are younger as you have more time to make up the losses; if you are older then invest in a higher percentage of safer stocks.

Don't put all your eggs in one basket – diversify to lower the risk.

Invest in the long term to maximise profit.

Review your portfolio on a regular basis as you might want to sell some stocks and buy others; as your circumstances change, then your stock portfolio should change.

Read the news and be informed; choose your shares based on the information you can gather about the companies you are interested in.

Finally, DON'T PANIC! Shares go up and down in price all the time; don't be tempted to buy or sell just because everybody else is!

If you follow the above rules then you should do well in the stock market overall over a long period of time. However, it is a gamble, and you need to be prepared to sometimes lose. This book should not be a replacement for financial advice from an expert. Whilst it should give you a good starting point it is recommended that you go and do further research into specific companies before you invest in anything. If you are stuck or not sure about an investment then don't part with any money until you have consulted an expert such as a stockbroker or a financial advisor.

A Short message from the Author:

Hey, are you enjoying the book? I'd love to hear your thoughts!

Many readers do not know how hard reviews are to come by, and how much they help an author.

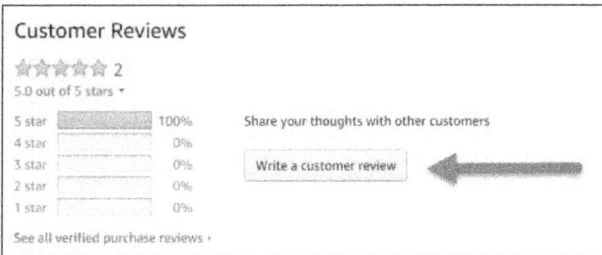

I would be incredibly thankful if you could take just 60 seconds to write a brief review on Amazon, even if it's just a few sentences!

You can leave a review under the Orders page, at the links below.

https://www.amazon.com/your-account
https://www.amazon.co.uk/your-account

Thank you for taking the time to share your thoughts!

www.ingramcontent.com/pod-product-compliance
Lightning Source LLC
Chambersburg PA
CBHW030518210326
41597CB00013B/947